THE
ROYAL
GLENS

THE
ROYAL
GLENS

ROBERT SMITH

JOHN DONALD PUBLISHERS LTD

EDINBURGH

To Sheila
who tramped the Royal Glens
with me

British Library Cataloguing in Publication Data
Smith, Robert, *1923 Apr, 18 –*
    The royal glens.
    1. Scotland. Highland Region, history
    I. Title
    941.15

ISBN 0 85976 316 1

Phototypeset by Newtext Composition Ltd, Glasgow
Printed and bound in Great Britain by Butler and Tanner, Frome, Somerset

CONTENTS

ACKNOWLEDGEMENTS

I would like to thank the staff of the Local History Department of Aberdeen Central Library for their invaluable assistance in researching this book, and also for the help given by the North East Scotland Library Service. I am grateful to Sheila Sedgwick for the Loinmuie poem, first published in an article she wrote for the *Deeside Field* magazine. Thanks also to Colin Gibson for permission to publish an extract from his book *Highland Deerstalker*. Finally, a word of thanks to all those other friendly folk who helped to guide me through the Royal Glens.

Robert Smith

The illustrations on the front and back covers are reproduced by courtesy of the Scotland in Focus Picture Library.

Location Map.

INTRODUCTION

WHEN IT WAS ALL OVER the Duke of Atholl said it had all been "one and twenty daft days". For three weeks the douce citizens of Edinburgh had wallowed in a sea of sentimentality, buried themselves under a mountain of tartan, and had their ear-drums shattered by the never-ending skirl of bagpipes – and all because of a man who was said by the essayist Leigh Hunt to be "a violator of his word, a libertine over head and ears in debt and disgrace, a man who has just closed half a century without one single claim on the gratitude of his country or the respect of posterity".

The year was 1822, and Auld Reekie had thrown away its inhibitions to welcome George IV, the first Hanoverian monarch to travel north of the border since the Duke of Cumberland had made his uninvited visit to Scotland less than a century before. They came from far and wide to see Royal Geordie, packing windows and doors, perching on rooftops, and risking life and limb on the tops of trees and walls. As one versifier, John Mayne, wrote –

> And a' the chieftains o' the North,
> Lords, leddies, lairds, and men of wirth,
> Are flocking to the frith o' Forth,
>   To welcome him, and a' that.

"Now the King's come!" exulted Sir Walter Scott in a poem of appalling bathos. The King *had* come, but reluctantly, for he was nagged by fears that "Butcher" Cumberland might have left some lasting scars, and nervous over the attitude of the Calvinistic Scots to his Royal morals. He was troubled about what they would say if his mistress, Lady Conyngham, accompanied him to Edinburgh, and when, in a fit of pique, she announced that she was spending August at Worthing and Hastings, he followed his usual custom of showering her with pearls and diamonds. She had, as Princess Dorothea Lieven remarked sarcastically, "an enormous balcony to wear them on".

The Royal knees, as well as Lady Conyngham's bosom, came in for criticism. When Geordie encased his gross figure in full Highland dress he wore flesh-coloured tights to cover his knees. "Since his stay will be so short," remarked Lady Saltoun tartly, "the more we see of him the better." There were also a number of rude ditties, including a verse inviting people "to kneel and kiss Royal Geordie's bum", but in the main the visit was a success.

Yet there was a fly in the ointment. Among all the hyperbole that oozed from writers' pens during the Royal visit, there was one passage referring to the King's

1

emotions "when he looked around and saw the distant Grampians". Royal Geordie, of course, was a long way from the Grampians, but many people thought he would go beyond the bounds of Edinburgh during his stay in Scotland. Mayne's "lords, leddies, lairds and men of worth" certainly expected it.

Lieutenant-Colonel Sir Evan Murray MacGregor, 19th Chief of Clan Gregor, believed that the King would travel through the country visiting the nobility. Some had even prepared their houses; the Duke of Montrose had instructed the architect John Nash to alter and extend his castle on Loch Lomondside. Even if a tour of the Highlands was not on the Royal itinerary, it was regarded as likely that the King would go to Taymouth Castle, home of the Marquis of Breadalbane, and to Blair to see the Duke of Atholl ("Old Ben-a'-Ghlo'," as Sir Walter Scott called him). In 1821, at a private audience, the King had told the Duke that he intended being in Scotland the following year and would "infallibly visit him". Now there was indecision, and the Duchess was irritated. Moreover, she had heard rumours that Lady Conyngham would be in the Royal party. If the King *did* visit Blair she would do her best, but she warned that the Duke's houses at Blair and Dunkeld were old and dirty and the furniture shabby. It would take two or three weeks to put them in a proper state to receive His Majesty. The problem never arose, for the King's ministers advised him not to travel beyond Edinburgh, which Sir Evan MacGregor found "quite inexplicable".

The King's visit to Scotland was his first and last. He never came back. Twenty years later, in 1842, another monarch stepped on to Scottish soil at Granton on her way to Edinburgh. She had been carried north by a converted man-of-war, a Royal yacht whose name sparked off memories of Geordie's trip. It was called the *Royal George*. Queen Victoria had arrived to take over where George IV had left off.

This time the Royal traveller was looking to the Grampians, setting off on a journey that would take her and Prince Albert from Edinburgh to Perth and on to the Highlands as guests of the Marquis of Breadalbane. This time, too, there would be a visit to the Duke of Atholl's home at Blair Castle, no longer, presumably, old and dirty. "The news," said *The Times*, "has flown from the capital to the provinces, wafted from tongue to tongue, through valley and glen, over mountain and moor, to the remotest corner of the highlands and islands."

Old Ben-a'-Ghlo's home at Blair was the spot from which Queen Victoria began her discovery of Scotland in the years that followed. It took her over the wild Drumochter Pass to Loch Laggan, along the silver length of the Spey, into Donside and the whisky glens of the Fiddich and the Livet, and up Deeside to her "Paradise" at Balmoral. Her carriage rumbled over roads that are now traffic-ridden highways, and through hamlets and villages that have burgeoned into bustling tourist communities, but Victoria went off the main routes, into the wilderness of glens and burns that stretches from the Spey to the Tay, from Atholl and the Monadhliath Mountains in the west to Strathdon and Strathmore in the east. She went on pony-back through the Feshie and the Tilt, Glen Clova and Glen Mark.

Later, the Queen was to go farther afield, on trips to Inverness and Glencoe,

Ballachulish and Ben Lomond, Dunrobin and Golspie, but it was the central area north of the Tay that held her captive. This was where her "Great Expeditions" took place, a vast mountainous landscape that was to become a sporting playground for those who followed ... Kings and Queens, Dukes and Duchesses, and the Lairds and their "leddies". Victoria set her seal on the Royal Glens, and the first shot fired by Prince Albert when he went deerstalking at Blair was like the crack of a starting pistol to sportsmen turning their eyes to the Scottish moors.

Shooting lodges were built in odd, out-of-the-way places, some of them incredibly sumptuous. The pampered sportsmen of the Victorian age liked their comforts when they went to the moors; one London firm offered to provide silver plate and "good reliable servants" at the lodges, while a Perth music seller had pianos for hire to any shooting lodge in Central Scotland. Times change. The lodges, or many of them, lie in ruins, but the shooting goes on. Shooting is big business now, with Germans and Americans footing huge bills for the privilege of shooting red deer. The Mar Lodge estate, where the Duke and Duchess of Fife once played host to Queen Victoria and the Prince of Wales (later Edward VII) on Deeside, was recently bought by an American billionaire called John Kluge. It is said that some 5,000 red deer roam the 77,500 acres of his estate. Mr Kluge's Royal neighbours frequently shoot over a number of Deeside estates.

So, this is the story of the Royal Glens. It begins on Deeside, goes by Strathdon to the Lecht and Tomintoul, and from there to the whisky glens of Speyside. It chases traffic along the A9, sidestepping from time to time into the Cairngorms, and tramps the Drumochter highway from Dalwhinnie to Dunkeld. Here, it turns east by the old passes to the Cairnwell and back to Deeside.

The ghosts of two centuries stalk these miles ... not only kings and queens, but ghillies and keepers, the lairds in their great houses, the whisky smugglers, the writers and road-builders, the artists who went into the glens with a paint brush in one hand and a gun in the other, the fiddlers who called the tune with their strathspeys and reels; and many more. But this is a book about the present as well as the past, showing the area as it is today, talking to the people who live on the edge of the wilderness, as well as in it, and marking the trails of the growing army of people who are following Royal footsteps through this awe-inspiring, lovely countryside.

*   *   *   *   *

Balmoral Castle, where Queen Victoria found her "dear Paradise". In 1848, when the Queen took up residence there, she walked with Prince Albert to a nearby hill and declared that the view was "charming".

Outside Balmoral Castle stands this bronze cast of a wild boar, the last on Deeside. From her room in the castle Queen Victoria could look down on this memento standing in her Rose Garden.

4

CHAPTER 1

GLEN

OF THE

PIGS

WHEN QUEEN VICTORIA FIRST CAME TO BALMORAL IN 1848, she fell in love with Glenmuick – "so wild and grand," she said – but she was less enthusiastic about its Gaelic name – *gleann muic*, the Glen of the Pigs. That was what the Gaels called it in the days when wild boar roamed the old Caledonian Forest. Victoria, who disliked the idea of part of her "dear Paradise" being called after pigs, wrote in her *Journal* that the name of the loch – *Muich* – meant "darkness" or "sorrow", but it was wishful thinking. The Gaelic word *muic* simply meant "pig".

Oddly enough, she had a permanent reminder of Glenmuick's pigs outside her window. From her room in Balmoral Castle, she looked down on a replica of the last wild boar on Deeside – a huge bronze cast standing in her Rose Garden. The Aberdeen photographer George Washington Wilson photographed it on one of his visits to Balmoral. When he was an art student in Aberdeen, Colin Gibson, the Dundee artist and writer, was summoned to Balmoral by King George V to colour the boar, along with a number of metal stags that ornamented the grounds. The King wanted to see them in their natural colours.

Colin got one of the house painters to bring him a stag's head from the castle corridors so that he could use it as a model. "I gave these stags the full treatment," he says, "the flashing eye, the red nostrils, the grass-stained teeth, the red-russet coat. It took me several days to complete them."

He thought the wild boar was "a real work of art". When he was half-way through painting it, storm clouds rolled over Lochnagar, threatening to ruin his efforts. Six gardeners came to the rescue. They laid a double line of planks over the grass, and, with sleety rain pelting down, lifted the boar on its pedestal and carried it to the carriage entrance in front of the castle, where he finished the job.

There was a sequel to his Balmoral adventure. Later, when he was in Florence as a travelling student, he found a replica of the Balmoral boar in the Mercato Nuovo. This one had water gushing from its mouth – it had been turned into a fountain. An inscription on the pedestal said it featured in a famous Hans Andersen story entitled "The Metal Pig". So, two pigs a world apart entertain the tourists, for Balmoral's boar is still there, glowering defiantly across the castle lawn.

Today only the deer run wild in the hills around Balmoral, and the name *gleann muic*, the Pigs' Glen, has ceased to have any meaning, but whatever its name, Glen Muick could probably claim to be the most popular glen in Scotland. It draws hundreds of visitors every year. It lies in the lap of Byron's "dark Lochnagar" and its river, the Muick, is the largest and best known tributary of the Dee. It has been the Royal Family's holiday home since Victoria discovered it a century and a half ago. "Of all the Dee's tributary glens," wrote Robert Anderson, author of *The Royal Dee*, in 1898, "that of the Muick is the finest. Well may it be called a Royal glen."

John Mitchell, who was there long before Royalty arrived, would have known all about wild boars. He lived at Dalfoury, not far from the Brig o' Muick, where the river tumbles into the Dee south of Ballater. There is a pool there that was known as Mitchell's Redd, a spawning ground for salmon. Mitchell, a skilful angler and a well-known poacher, died in the early eighteenth century and was buried in the Brig o' Muick kirkyard, only a stone's throw from where he slipped out at night to gaffe his

The Queen Mother leaving Glenmuick Parish Church, Ballater. By courtesy of Aberdeen Journals Ltd.

illegal salmon. Curious sightseers come to peer at the coffin-shaped slab over his grave, for the dates on it – 1596 to 1722 – show that he lived to the exceptional age of 126. A poem found in the fly-leaf of an old book is said to have been written by him. In it, he described how he was a bachelor for forty years, married for twenty-six years, widowed for three, and married again for fifty-five years:

> Between my cradle and my grave, I wean,
> Seven monarchs and two queens have been.
> Twice Presbyt'ry gave way to Stuart gowns;
> As oft again thrust out prelatic lowns.

The Glenmuick of Mitchell's lifetime was a vastly different place from the sparsely-populated glen of today. If he had written about it in his poem, he would have pictured it alive with people. There were settlements scattered throughout the glen from Bridge-end to the Spittal – the "Spittelhauche", as it was called in 1600. The names can still be seen on early maps and in old records … Stoddart Croft, sometimes called Stoiter, Knockandhu, Bog, Rinasluick, the cattle-run of the slabs, Balnoe, Byallachur, Toildow or Toldhu, the black hole, and Clashmuick, the pigs' furrow – another reminder of the pig days.

The ruins of these old settlements are strewn about the moors only a short distance from the road, the old Glenmuick running parallel with the new. Aberdeen archaeologists Ian A.G. Shepherd and Sandra M. Ralston carried out a survey of these sites a number of years ago, putting pieces of the jigsaw together, so that the untidy clutter of stones now take shape as living communities. Behind the farm of Aultonrea were six longhouses and two kailyards, while up on Garlot Hill and elsewhere are the lines of run-rig farming.

On the south-facing slope of Auchnacraig Hill, almost opposite the Linn of Muick, there was a small township consisting of five longhouses and an enclosure, and another township of four longhouses nearby. The *larachs* lie in a green, sheltered bowl cut off from the rest of the glen. Eight tenants lived in this tiny Shangri-la in the Deeside hills.

Perhaps the most interesting site is Blar Charriad, a name that, intriguingly, means "field of conflicts". It was shown on an 1869 map as Balacariag, but it eventually became known as Blacharrage. Even in the late nineteenth century it was "in ruins", yet here, more than anywhere else in Glenmuick, I felt as if I was actually walking through a recognisable township. Balacaraig was said to be "a substantial township of twelve houses, three enclosures and a corn-drying kiln". The kiln is still there, and the sinuous patterns of run-rigs stand out quite clearly. This settlement is linked with another shown on the 1869 map as Loinmore, where there were five houses.

The map also shows a track running across the moor from Loinmore to a hill road climbing up from the Bridge of Muick and Balintober. Queen Victoria went this way when she rode "up the peat-road over the hill of Polach" on her way south to Mount Keen and Glen Mark in 1861. The route by the Pollagach Burn was known as the Pollach Road.

Some of the settlements have vanished. Loinmuie, lying below the Craig of Loinmuie on the left bank of the Muick, has been swallowed up by Allcailleach Forest. Sheila Sedgewick, who lives in Glen Girnock and has researched this Deeside corner from old kirk records, discovered that there were four families of crofters at Loinmuie. An old poem which she came upon mentions three of these families – Stewart (alias Dowie), Lachlan and Riach. There was no indication of when this nostalgic verse was written, but already depopulation had laid a ravaging hand on the land:

> Those days are gone, those pleasures past,
> Those friends will meet nae mair.
> Now ruined walls and the moaning blast
> Where once stood Granny's chair;
> Where happy families once were seen
> Of 'Lachlans', 'Riachs', and 'Dowie'.
> The thistle waves and grass grows green
> O'er homes around Loinmuie.

The Stewarts were prominent in Glen Muick in the seventeenth and eighteenth centuries, having been given a wadset (mortgage) of the lands of Aucholzie in 1680. This included Auchnacraig, Stodartcroft, and Bellino (Balnoe). There were six tenants in Aucholzie towards the end of the seventeenth century and eight in Auchnacraig.

The Stewarts were allied by marriage to the McHardies of Crathie and Crathienaird, who were "a wild and extravagant race", and together they "gave much trouble to their neighbours". William Stewart, who owned Aucholzie in 1715, was certainly regarded as a troublemaker. In 1704, his name appeared in a list of "Apostats, Popish Priests, Papists and their children". He had apparently renounced "the errors of poperie", but nine months later, as the authorities crudely put it, "scandalously returned to his vomite". He took part in the 1715 Rising and died about 1727.

From 1750, the Gordons occupied Aucholzie for over a century. The name means "the field of the wood", and it can still be seen on a wooden sign at the end of a farm track on the glen road, about a mile from the Linn. The farm buildings are deserted. In time, the sign will go, so that all that will be left to remind us of Aucholzie will be the lines of an old Ballad:

> At the head o' the Etnach the battle began,
> At Little Aucholzie they killed their first man.
> They killed William Gordon and James o' the Knock,
> And brave Alexander, the flower o' Glenmuick.

"The Baron of Braickley" is the story of how John Farquharson of Inverey, the famous Black Colonel, slew John Gordon of Brackley in an encounter that took place following a dispute over fines for the killing of black-fish. Etnach is in Glen Tanar, so if the ballad is to be believed the "battle" raged over the hills between the Muick and the Tanar. The setting is also mentioned in part of the ballad in which Peggy, the wife of John

Aucholzie means "the field of the wood". The farm buildings are now deserted, but there were Stewarts here in the seventeenth and eighteenth centuries, and from 1750 the Gordons occupied Aucholzie for over a century.

Gordon, dances and sings with joy at her husband's death. She advises Farquharson to flee through Birse and Aboyne – "out o'er a' the hills o' Glentanar you'll skip in an hour".

Glenmuick ends at the Spittal, but a few hundred yards from the crowded car park and visitors' centre there is a rickle of stones at the roadside which gets little attention from passing motorists. This is all that is left of Titaboutie, where Ian Shepherd and Sandra Ralston found traces of two longhouses. The name has always been a puzzle, but it would be true to say that nobody "teets" or looks very closely at the site now.

Yet Titaboutie is another reminder of the folk who lived out their lives in this once-remote glen. A schoolhouse stood near Titaboutie, and as far back as 1740 the Society in Scotland for Propagating Christian Knowledge established a school at Balnoe, where there were sixty pupils – thirty-seven boys and twenty-three girls. There was also a school at the Mill of Sterin, one of eight schools in the parish last century.

Titaboutie boasted a public house until 1815, when it was moved to the Spittal, near the ancient hospice. Here, drovers rested their cattle by the Allt-Darrarie before driving them over the Capel Mount to Glen Clova, and crowds of Highland shearers, men and women on their way over the Mount to harvest crops in the south, broke their journey at the Spittal and spent the night in barns and outhouses. There are said to be mounds and cairns on the banks of the Allt Darrarie marking the graves of travellers who took the old route over the Capel ... a packman murdered for his purse, a shepherd who perished in the snow in 1843, a "souter" who informed on whisky smugglers and paid the penalty, a party of umbrella-menders who lost their lives in a storm.

The railways came, the roads improved, and there were no more drovers and thravers. By the middle of last century most of the hill traffic had gone. In 1846, the hostelry at the Spittal, like the hospice before it, disappeared. Now only hunters and hill-walkers cross the Capel, as well as the occasional enthusiast on a mountain bike, following the pioneering steps – or cycle tracks – of sixteen people who pedalled over the Capel in 1892, becoming the first cyclists to cross the Mounth from Glen Muick to Glen Clova.

In 1863, Glen Muick was bought by Sir James McKenzie, the son of an Aberdeen silk merchant, who made a fortune in India. He lived in Glenmuick House, a huge building described by the writer Nigel Tranter as "a great sham-Tudor edifice", but it was eventually demolished. Sir James, who bought Glen Muick as a sporting estate, added the Bachnagairn beat to it, which, along with the Spittal beat, was added to Balmoral estate by King George VI between 1947 and 1951. In 1974, in conjunction with the Scottish Wildlife Trust, the Balmoral estate established the present 6,350-acre nature reserve.

When the nature reserve was set up, there were fears that it would destroy the very thing that drew people to the hills. So far, this hasn't happened, although the car park can no longer cope with the weekend crowds. Cars spill out and line the edge of the moor almost as far back as Titaboutie. The people most affected by the change are members of the Royal Family. Glass-allt Shiel is still used by guests from Balmoral, but "the Royals" are rarely seen there, and certainly not when the tourist season is at its height. Allt-na-guibhsaich – "The Hut" of Queen Victoria's day – lies empty most of the year.

Gone are the days when Balmoral house parties descended on Loch Muick for a day's fishing. One of these Royal picnics, laid on by King Edward VII, was described by Colin Gibson in his book, *Highland Deer Stalker*, the story of Allan Cameron, a Glen Muick deer stalker:

Two boats were used on Loch Muick by Royal fishers in the years before the war, one for carrying people up the loch, the other for angling. "These fishing parties were good fun," wrote Colin Gibson, the writer and artist. "The trout were small. To augment the basket, the stalkers and some of their guests usually made a sweep or two with a net, keeping the best fish 'for the pot,' and returning the others." The picture above, which hangs in the home of Miss Mabel Gordon, formerly housekeeper at Birkhall, shows King George V; Miss Gordon's father, Frank Gordon, head stalker; and the Duke of York, later King George VI. This unique photograph was taken in the early 1930s.

Balmoral had two boats – a heavy one, six-oared, and used for transport along the three miles of the loch, and a flat-bottomed coble for angling. Glenmuick had one boat, housed down at the Spittal end. These fishing parties were good fun, but nobody took the fishing very seriously. A few rowed over to the islet, while the majority walked round to the head of the loch and fished from the bank. The trout were small. To augment the basket, the stalkers and some of the guests usually made a sweep or two with a net, keeping the best fish 'for the pot', and returning the others.

Allan lent a hand at the netting. Uncle Sandy (Alexander Cameron, a stalker at Allt-na-guibhsaich) was there, supervising operations, or ghillying for Queen Alexandra when she had a try with the rod. The two kilted grandsons (later King Edward VIII and King George VI) spent most of their time wading in the shallows and guddling under stones, ably directed by the King himself.

Prince Arthur Connaught (young and handsome in the kilt) and a Mr Hervey (who always carried telescope and walking stick) were energetic members of the party, but General Dighton Probyn and Sir David Nairne Welch, K.C.V.O., C.V.O., M.V.O., who was a retired captain and had commanded the Royal Yachts *Fairy* and *Alberta* from 1848 to 1878, preferred to take things easy. The Captain was a little gnome-like man, and even in the sunshine he wore an overcoat. Sir Dighton looked very dignified – even on a fishing picnic – with his long white beard, black knickerbocker suit and chimney-pot hat. Princess May (later Queen Mary) and Lady Katherine Coke were often in the fishing party.

Today the Royal Family head for other pastures ... up on to the Capel plateau hunting the deer and grouse, while army guards keep walkie-talkie watch from the Sandy Hillock huts; through Ballochbuie Forest (Victoria called it "the bonniest plaid in Scotland") to a shiel where Prime Minister Harold Wilson had tea with the Queen and Mary Wilson helped her to dry the dishes; and along a dusty path to Gelder Shiel, in the shadow of Lochnagar, where an inscription above the door carries the date 1865 and reads "Ruidh na Bhan Righ" – the Shieling of the Queen. Here, Victoria had tea and brown trout with Empress Eugénie of France.

It is still the Shieling of the Queen, but now a wooden patio has been built outside the door so that today's Royal picnickers can barbecue their trout. Across the path is the stable, which was long ago opened up to hillwalkers as a howff in which to shelter from the storms of Lochnagar. From Gelder a track trails away west from the Feith an Laoigh, a stream that comes tumbling down from Feith Ord, or Feithort as Victoria called it, past the Prince's stone. The barely readable inscription on the stone says that Prince Albert spent a night there when out hunting, but, in fact, he sheltered in what the Queen called "a little 'housie' – not at all uncomfortable".

Near the main track, where a narrow path turns uphill to Feith Ord, I came upon a hitching post which Prince Charles uses when out riding. It is more than likely that he leaves his pony there and climbs up Feith Ord to sit at the stone where another Royal Prince slept the night away after shooting three stags. As he rides over the old tracks around Balmoral, Prince Charles must often think of the Queen who explored these same hills and glens on ponyback so many years ago.

East of Glen Gelder is little-known Glen Girnock, which had more illicit whisky stills than any other glen on Deeside, so it is not surprising that the Royal Lochnagar Distillery sits on Girnock's doorstep. A track from the distillery meets up with a track from Littlemill and runs past Caistel na Caillich, the castle of the old woman or witch, east of Lochnagar. It comes out on the Muick at Inchnabobart, once a farm, now a Royal lodge, beautifully furnished and decorated.

The last of the Royal glens in this area takes its name from the River Gairn –

Dark Lochnagar … and the loch which gave the mountain its name. Hundreds of people climb it during the year, many of them unaware that it can be a temperamental and dangerous hill. Byron immortalised it with his lines about "the tempests of dark Lochnagar".

garbh-abhainn, the rough stream, the longest tributary of the Dee. It rises on the summit of Ben Avon and runs for twenty miles to join the Dee at what has always been known simply as the Fit o' Gairn, just outside Ballater. Near the ruined church of Glengairn is St Mungo's Well and at one time a fair was held on the hillside at Abergairn. There was an old superstition that if you didn't attend the feast of St Mungo at the Fit o' Gairn you wouldn't live till the following year.

Myth and mystery bred easily in the Land of Gairn. The farms and holdings scattered about Gairnside go back to an age when superstition was rampant – "the auld chiel", as one priest called Old Nick, was never very far from your shoulder. Ghosts were seen in the Glack o' Morven and lights flickered in the kirkyard when a death was imminent – corpse's candles, they called them. Father Lachlan McIntosh, who was a priest at Ardoch early last century, was walking through a wood when a "pyat" (magpie) kept landing on his shoulder. "Pyats" were birds of ill omen and that night Father

Her Majesty the Queen visits the Albert Memorial Hall, Ballater. The police sergeant
stands to attention in period costume. Courtesy of Aberdeen Journals Ltd.

McIntosh heard that his nephew had murdered a girl near Crathie. He was later hanged
for it in Aberdeen.

Ardoch was a hamlet with about fourteen "fire-houses" – houses with chimneys. It
was "a nasty guttery (muddy) place". "The hooses in Ardoch was stragglin' back an' fore
as if they had fa'an oot o' the air," said one resident. They had a school there, but it was
"just a reeky hole". It is still a guttery place. The track that runs along the slopes of
Mammie to Ardoch is lined with the ruins of the "fire-houses", but there is nothing to
tell which was the school, the "reeky hole". The only building left is Ardoch itself, but
it has become a shell, its empty windows staring sightlessly across the Gairn to Geallaig
Hill.

There is another Ardoch in the south-west corner of Geallaig Hill, under Creag a'
Chlamhain, near Crathie. Rob Bain has a sheep farm there. From his front door he
looks over the rooftops of Balmoral Castle to the upper reaches of the Dee and east to
the corries of Lochnagar.

Rob, who is sixty, has been there for over fifty years. He was born in Braemar, but when he was only six weeks old he was taken to live at the remote farm of Dalownie in Glengairn. He is a bit of a character, untroubled by the niceties of life. He grins his toothless grin and jokes, "I've got twa teeth an' my dog has one e'e."

People come to Ardoch to look at the view. Some are newspaper photographers out for a "shot" at the castle. Rob came home one day to find a party of Italian newspapermen *inside* his house. He chased them down the hill.

Geallaig, the white hill, rises between the Dee and the Gairn. King Edward VII used to shoot over Geallaig, riding up the quarry road on a pony with his Inverness cape wrapped about him. He liked to act like one of the locals, talking to them in their North-east tongue. Once, meeting a retired ghillie called Peter Robertson, who had been with him at Abergeldie Castle, he went up to him, shook his hand, and asked in broad Doric: "Man, Peter, foo are ye?"

The name Mammie has a more maternal ring to it, but all that it means is the little round hill. "Thacket hoosies" clung to it as if hiding away from the domination of Morven, *mor bheinn*, the big hill. This scattered community is cushioned by hills –

Ardoch was once a hamlet of fourteen houses. All that now remains is the shell of the building of Ardoch itself, facing towards Geallaig Hill.

Mammie, the Lary, Torbeg, the Brown Cow Hill, which some say looks more like a whale than a "broon coo", and the curiously named Ca', over which the drovers took their cattle on their way south from Corgarff.

The Rev. Thomas Meany, a Roman Catholic priest, who served there from 1888 to 1899, listened to the tales of his Gairnside parishioners and jotted them down in two ruled exercise books … stories about fights and fairies, peat-casting on the priest's moss-day, cock-fighting and whisky smuggling in Glen Fenzie.

Cock-fighting was a great event in the Gairnside calendar. Each pupil brought a cock to school and the defeated cocks, called "fugies", were claimed by the dominie. Father Meany's account of this bloody sport came from Lewie Mackenzie – Lewie of the Laggan – who said that the best fighter was called the King, the second the Queen, and the third the Knave. "What waps (blows) they did gie," declared Lewie.

The Gairnsiders themselves were good at giving "waps". They often clashed with men from the other glens, particularly the "Tarland tykes", who had a defiant saying, "Gairnside, for a' yer pride, Tarland winna fear ye". Gairnside's womenfolk were as tough as their men. A burly Amazon called Meg Riach often waded in when the going got rough. "Meg gaed ahint the Gairnside men wi' a stick, skirling at them, 'Ye Gairnside men, keep roon thegither an' strike clean'. She wiz a gey hardy billie, wiz Meg, a terrible woman and a great smuggler. She saved heaps o' fowk wi' her strength."

Meg liked a dram with the best of them and there was an amusing tale about what happened on the day of her mother's funeral. "Her mither died in Glenfinzie in the days o' the great storm and they had to cam' wi' the body by the heid o' Mammie to the churchyard o' Dalfad. They found the grave fu' o' watter and Meg was fa'in aneath the coffin – she was maybe the waur o' drink."

Across the Glenfenzie Burn is Inverenzie, where Robert Shaw, the Highland heavyweight, practised putting the stone and throwing the caber in the years before the last war. Up-river, the hump-backed Gairnshiel bridge loups the Gairn water and carries the military road north to Tornahaish and Corgarff, a smooth, tarmacadam road now, but a rough, twisting track not so many years ago. Near the bridge is Gairnshiel Lodge, now a hotel, and a short distance downstream is Dalphuil, the Old Schoolhouse. Queen Elizabeth the Queen Mother bought it in 1938 for the little princesses. It was shaped like an old-fashioned teapot and that's what it was called – the Teapot Cottage.

Behind the larachs and the dead stones are the fading memories of the people who lived there, generations of Gairnside folk who played out their lives in this once-thriving community. Amy Stewart Fraser, whose book, *The Hills of Home*, became a best-seller and put Glengairn on the map, wrote about the "Gaun-aboot-Bodies" on Gairnside, the tinkers and pedlars whose comings and goings, like autumn leaves or the first bright budding of blossom in spring, marked the changing of the seasons … Besom Charlie, who made birch brooms from bundles of twigs and pot-rinsers from heather, Charlie Wood, who peddled boot-laces and matches and was inevitably known as Charlie Timmer, and Mackie the Pig Man, who not only sold crockery but exchanged it

All that remains of the remote manse of Tullochmacarrick, once part of a hamlet of six or eight cottages.

Another manse which has gone to ruin is that of Dalfad where Amy Stewart Fraser, author of *The Hills of Home*, was born. The picture below shows all that remains of the old Dalfad kirkyard.

George Mackie feeds his sheep at Delnabo, near Gairnshiel.

for rabbit- and hare-skins. Sometimes he paid for the skins with a plate or a pudding basin.

Life ebbs out of the glen as you go west from Gairnshiel. Above a wooden bridge crossing the Gairn is the farm of Tullochmacarrick, deserted like so many others, and not far away, along an old track to Gairnshiel, is another ruin, all that is left of the minister's house. It was a two-storey building, looking down on a hamlet of six or eight cottages, and it was to this remote manse that the Rev. Robert Neil brought his bride in 1847. Later, he moved to a new manse at Dalfad, near the old burial ground, and in 1891 his successor, the Rev. James Lowe, moved in. He was Amy Stewart Fraser's father.

Glengairn is locked into the past. There is little for visitors apart from the scenery, the only attractions being home baking at Gairnshiel Lodge and an art gallery, the McEwan Gallery, near the Fit o' Gairn. The kirk where Robert Neil and James Lowe preached is still opened occasionally for services and the neighbouring school is now a private home, but there is a pervading sense of desolation in the glen. "Perhaps such places have had their day," wrote another daughter of the manse, Catherine G. Neil, in *Glengairn Calling!* That was many years ago, and even then she was regretting the sight of "one house after another being pulled down".

The demolition of her father's manse at Tullochmacarrick caused "great regret and

18

indignation" among the folk of the glen, but the manse at Dalfad, where Amy Stewart Fraser was born, has also gone. All that is left is a heap of rubble near an old, red-roofed steading – and the memory of a garden "full of old-fashioned flowers, pyrethrums, monk's hood, bachelor's buttons, Canterbury bells, peonies, and the gloriously heavy-scented pheasant-eye narcissus".

It was here, in what had been the glebe, that I came on George Mackie feeding his sheep. George and his wife Norma came north from Glen Lethnot eighteen years ago to take over the sheep farm at Delnabo, near Gairnshiel. They knew Amy Stewart Fraser well. Some years ago, before she died, she wanted to see the Queen Mother's shiel at Auchtavan in lonely Glen Fearder. The Mackies took her there, turning the trip into a nostalgic journey that covered much of the countryside she knew and loved.

It took them along the Gairn to Loch Builg, past Corndavon Lodge, which in Amy's childhood was let to Lord Cardigan, of Crimean fame, and to Loinahaun, once the house of an old weaver. His wife was related to John Brown, and on one occasion Queen Victoria drove up to their thatched cottage in her carriage, drawn by grey horses and led by an outrider. Brown's folk were proud of their relative, although a bit sceptical of his role in the affairs of State. "Oor Jock maun hae a devilish good heid tae manage a' the affairs o' the nation," remarked one of them sardonically.

The Queen gave gifts of shawls and tea and tobacco to the old couple at Loinahaun and then the Royal carriage drove away up the glen, past Daldownie, where they always came to the door to wave to her Majesty when she passed that way. Daldownie was a

The Royal Shiel at Auchtavan in Glen Fearder. Beyond it is Auchnagymlinn, where Deeside's first licensed still is thought to have operated.

Corndavon Lodge which, in Amy Stewart Fraser's childhood, was let to Lord Cardigan, of Crimean War fame.

sheep farm and the man who lived there firmly believed in fairies. He had heard their revels during the night and had seen the marks of their footsteps in the morning. The ruinous building stood untouched for a number of years, but finally it was demolished. There are no more fairy footprints in the dawn dew.

The Gairn track runs out under the rocky ramparts of Ben Avon, where the Bealach Dearg – the Red Pass – trails north from Invercauld on its way to Inchrory and Tomintoul. Other tracks come creeping out of the heather, over the east shoulder of Culardoch, the highest hill between the Gairn and the Dee, and from the empty acres of Aberarder, where John Brown's mother, Margaret Leys, was born, the daughter of a blacksmith.

This is a cold and desolate spot. Donald McHardy, a stalker, lived with his wife and family in Lochbuilg Lodge. The lodge, now a ruin, stood on a knoll overlooking Lochan Feurach and Lochan Orr, two of the group of tiny lochans that mark the parting of the ways for the Bealach Dearg and the road to Gairnside.

There is a rickety boathouse on the edge of the loch. The first time I was there a Glenfiddich whisky bottle hung by a string from the rafters – empty. There was also a woollen jersey on the line with the word "Emergency" written across it. Someone had left a message for all the weary hill folk who come down from the heights of Ben A'an to shelter in this draughty howff. It was chalked across the wall in large white letters. "Welcome to the highest boathouse in the country," it said. "Peace and love to you all."

CHAPTER 2

A
FEARFUL
HILL

T HE WORDS OF THE "EDOM O' GORDON" BALLAD hang like a shroud over the sixteenth century keep-tower of Corgarff:

> Oh, bonnie, bonnie was her mouth,
> And cherry were her cheeks
> And clear, clear was her yellow hair,
> Whereon the reid bluid dreeps.

Haunted by these mournful lines, Corgarff Castle nurses its secrets at the foot of the notorious Lecht Pass in Upper Donside. In 1571, when a tragic feud between the

The remains of one of the bridges on the old military road to Corgarff.

Gordon and Forbes clans was played out in this remote corner of Aberdeenshire, the castle was burned to the ground. Twenty-seven people died. One version of the ballad says that the daughter of the house was killed while being lowered down the castle wall, another that the laird's wife and family died in the fire – "baith ladye and babes were brent (burnt)".

Here, where the wind "blew shrill and cauld" on that terrible day, the old hill tracks spin out like the gossamer threads of a spider's web. From Corgarff, they run west by the Royal lodge at Delnadamph to Inchrory, reaching out to the distant Cairngorms; south by the Cock Burn to Glengairn, and east by Delachuper and Delavine to Deeside. The Delachuper path, with its crumbling Wade bridges, was the main link between Deeside and Donside, part of the old military road going north from Crathie to Tomintoul. Before it was built in the mid-eighteenth century, an Ensign Rutherford, stationed at Corgarff, described how an earlier track crossed the River Don half a mile below Corgarff, passed through a village called "Milnetown of Allairg", went over the hill of Allairg, and then rose over "a high mountain call'd the Lecht".

Two centuries later, the infamous Lecht still taunts and torments its travellers. It is one of the best-known roads in the country, and mostly for the wrong reasons. For years, winter road reports have carried the familiar message: "The road from Cock Bridge to Tomintoul is closed". There is a story told about a man who travelled over the Lecht in the summer and landed at the Allargue Arms Hotel (the "Briggies") at half-past two in the morning. The lights were still burning in the bar and when he went in he found it doing a roaring trade. "When do you close?" asked the surprised visitor. "Och!" said the publican, glancing at the clock, "usually about December."

It may not have been far from the truth, for at one time you could take it for granted that, come the turn of the year, the storm-bound Lecht would be closed to traffic for weeks on end. The record was set in 1961–62, when it was closed for 118 days. Unless you have lived there, or sheltered in the Briggies when snow spears the air at the foot of the Lecht, you can have little idea of what life can be like in this raw North-east corner. I remember Isobel Conboy, who lives at Ordacoy, telling me that when she came to Corgarff ten years ago she found that if you were careless you could die within a few yards of your own front door.

Wullie Gray, the Bard of Corgarff, knows all about storms on the Lecht. His sheep farm at the Luib is opposite the Milltown track and his "beat" covers 30,000 acres, stretching north to the Lecht ski slopes and across bleak moorland to the Braes of Glenlivet. When he isn't looking after 600 sheep he scribbles dialect poetry on the backs of old envelopes and recites them to audiences at the Briggies. "Winter's early, Spring is late", went a line in one of his poems. It told of how he had to dig for black faced ewes "buried deep in the drifts o' snaw".

The last time I saw Wullie he was coming down the Hill of Allargue by the old road from the Lecht, with his dog Rusty. The first snow of winter had fallen, and Wullie was penning some of his sheep beside an old shepherd's cottage at the Milltown. The Milltown of today looks little like the community mentioned by Ensign Rutherford.

Wullie Gray, "the Bard of Corgarff", famous for his dialect poetry, but seen here with his collie dog, Rusty.

There are only two buildings there now, Auchmore, the white house up on the hill, and Milltown Cottage.

So what happened to the village? "That," said Wullie, pointing to a heap of rubble across the track, "was the shoppie, and this," indicating the mound of stones he was standing on, "was the cobbler's shop." Auchmore was "the cairter's hoose", and the meal mill was on the main track, still in good condition. The "miller's place" was higher up the Milltown Burn.

The Milltown Burn stirs sad memories. More than a century ago, a girl called Margaret Cruickshank, who worked as housekeeper at Milltown, lost her way in a blizzard and, instead of following the Milltown Burn, which would have taken her to her own doorstep, went east by the Ernan Burn and died. Her story was told in a ballad, "Lassie o' the Lecht," written by James Ferguson, a baker at Bridge of Avon, in Upper Banffshire, and sung in farm kitchens and bothies all over the North-east. When I was talking about it to Wullie at Milltown, saying how only a short distance had separated her from safety, he remarked, "It's a big operation getting from here to the Luib on a day o' drift". The Luib is less than half a mile away.

I left Wullie and went up the Hill of Allargue, following the long-forgotten trail tramped by the soldiers from Corgarff Castle. Up there, the hills were glittering white and dimpled with shadow, stretching away to Inchrory and Ben Avon. Down below, the woods of Delnadamph stood out against a gleaming blanket of snow, and in the

The Lecht Cairn commemorates Margaret Cruickshank, who, more than a century ago, lost her way in a blizzard and died.

distance I could pick out the silhouette of Lochnagar. Then, as I crossed the plateau, the dark line of the Lecht road came in sight, soaring upwards, paced by a marching line of electric pylons.

"This fearful hill", Queen Victoria called the Lecht when she went over it on her way to Glen Fiddich in 1850. There isn't a year when it is free of snow, but some years are worse than others. The year 1937 was a bad one. It was said that at Corgarff the tops of telephone poles stuck out of the snow like paling posts, while up in Glenbuchat the houses were buried so deep that only the "lums" were clear. People remember seeing dogs playing around the chimneys of Glenbuchat House. Down at Corgarff there is a reminder of that grim winter in a broken slab in the local kirkyard. The inscription on it reads "A Man Unknown", and the date is given as May 3, 1937. The dead man's body was found in the Lecht in the Spring. Nobody was reported missing, and they never found out who he was. Some said he must have been a tinker.

Next to the Man Unknown there is an even more poignant reminder of the toll that the Lecht can take – the grave of Margaret Cruickshank. The faded inscription on it tells how she "perished on the Lecht on February 4, 1860, aged 19 years". More than five hundred men searched the hills for her, without success. Her body was found three months later by a young shepherd in Glen Ernan. Today, like the ballad, the Lassie o' the Lecht is forgotten. Not many see her gravestone in Corgarff kirkyard; fewer still know of the "Lassie o' the Lecht" cairn, which stands on a lonely plateau above the Ernan Water.

The Lecht hills have always been hungry for victims, but there was no hint of that long-forgotten tragedy when I went up Glen Ernan in the Spring. Wild flowers were bursting into life along the track and the words of the "Lassie o' the Lecht" were still fresh in my mind ... " from each hillside the smile o' May had chased the winter snow away".

These lovely Strathdon glens play Cinderella to Deeside's Royal glens, but it would be easy to argue a historical case that Donside should also be dubbed Royal. John Buchan once described the Don as the Loire of Scotland, and it lacks nothing in ancient castles, mighty battles and long-forgotten legends.

It has its own beauty. As you go west through Strathdon towards the Lecht, the names of the glens become a prayerful litany ... Glenkindie, Glenbuchat, Glen Ernan, Glen Nochty. The Strathdon glens belong to a way of life that has all but disappeared. The great houses, or those that are left, speak of a more elegant age, when Queen Victoria had her tartan made on a loom at Clashnettie and the men of Lonach marched over the hills to the Braemar Gathering and marched back through Balmoral. "They stopped and cheered three-times-three, throwing up their bonnets," wrote the Queen. When the Royal ghillies saw the Lonach men coming they volunteered to carry them over the River Dee. It was, said Victoria, "worthy of chivalrous times".

The chivalrous times, like some of the great houses, have gone. Glenbuchat Castle, whose rebellious Jacobite laird – "de great Glenbogget" – gave George II nightmares, is a ruin, and Castle Newe (pronounced Nyow), where Queen Mary climbed into an attic to look at an electric chicken brooder invented by the laird, Sir Charles Forbes, was pulled down more than sixty years ago. Built by John Forbes ("Bombay Jock", who founded the family fortunes in India), it was designed by Archibald Simpson, its highest tower topping that of Balmoral Castle. The same curious, rectangular chimneys that rose above the onion-shaped tourelles of the castle can be seen, oddly out of place, in the buildings at Bellabeg, as well as above the two quaint lodge cottages at the entrance to Glen Nochty.

Glen Ernan and Glen Nochty are two of the loveliest glens in Strathdon. One of the big mansion houses in the wooded acres of Glen Nochty was Auchernach, built for the Forbes family in 1819 and later occupied by George F. Rose, of Rose's Lime fame. He was a man who liked to have the best people at his table. One of his visitors was Scott Skinner, the Strathspey King, who composed a tune while staying at Auchernach. The House of Auchernach has gone, but behind the rubble that lies on the site a series of broken stone steps leads into a huge walled garden. Locked away in this corner of Tornashean Forest, this secret garden draws you back to the time when General Charles Forbes, Barrack Master at Corgarff, lived there, and when, in later years, George Rose

The House of Auchernach has gone, but behind remains a huge walled garden, overgrown now, containing this lofty crenellated tower.

Scott Skinner, the Strathspey King, was a visitor at Auchernach. He is portrayed here by David Waterson. By courtesy of the National Galleries of Scotland.

met his shooting guests at the door with a glass of whisky in his hand, ready to "damp the doorstep" for them.

It is wild and unruly now, overgrown with weeds, full of prickling nettles and savage thistles, and here, in this chaos of bush and flower, a willow tree weeps for the past over what was known as Napoleon's Well. The twentieth century laid siege to Auchernach, but the garden looks as if it had been made to withstand any assault on its tranquillity. Two circular towers are built into its high walls and at the far end of the garden there is a lofty crenellated tower that might have been plucked from one of Bombay Jock's hill forts in India. Did Mr Rose sit here and drink his gin and lime while looking down on his Secret Garden?

Hidden in the woods behind the garden are other buildings belonging to the estate, including a tower with a weather vane cock on top of it, testing the winds that come whistling down from the Loops of Badenyon in Glenbuchat. The land at Auchernach belongs to the Forestry Commission. I heard that a local farmer had been talking about clearing and replanting the garden, so perhaps the days of Auchernach's

Hillwalkers pause at Duff's Defiance. This, says one account, is where a local man defied the gaugers with his illicit still. Another story is that a squatter defied the local laird by building his house here, across the boundaries of three estates.

glory may return. Back in 1914 a horse-drawn railway was built to take timber out of the Forest of Auchernach. It ran from Aldachuie to just south of Torrancroy, but it was dismantled in 1919.

The highest inhabited house in the glen is at Aldachuie. Peter Goodfellow, a commercial artist, lives there with his wife Jean. The first thing that greets you at Aldachuie is a huge wooden sculpture on the track near the front door, and another in a nearby field. Peter bought the wooden sculpture when it was exhibited at Kildrummy Castle, and the second work was being "stored" for a friend. He comes from Teesside. The house at Aldachuie has changed hands a number of times in recent years, and Peter said that the previous owners had all been English. Half the glens in Scotland have been invaded by Englishmen, but Peter and his wife deserve their corner in Strathdon. They searched long and hard for their little bit of Paradise, and when they came upon Glen Nochty they knew that they had found it.

Beyond Aldachuie, I headed for the Ladder Hills, keeping an eye open for Duff's

Defiance, which is marked on the Ordnance Survey map. This was where a local man defied the gaugers with his illicit still. The ruins of his house are on the edge of a burn at the foot of the Hill of Aldachuie. There are contradictory stories about Duff's Defiance. The whisky story is the more popular one, but there is another tale that a man called Lucky Thain came over the hills from Glenlivet and squatted there, defying the local laird, a Duff. He is said to have built his house across the boundaries of three estates, so that the frustrated Duff was unable to demolish the house.

Both stories may be true, for the lairds were strongly opposed to illicit whisky-making. John Milne's poem, "Noughty Glens", which described the battles between whisky smugglers and gaugers, said that the Excisemen were sent out by Lord Fife and other proprietors – "our gentlemen surveyed the hills, and sore destroyed the smuggling stills." Duff was the family name of the Earl of Fife, who had a hunting lodge called Backies near the old castle of Badenyon.

The Earl may have been following the example of Sir Charles Forbes of Newe, who refused to grant leases to tenants found guilty of smuggling. Illicit distilling wasn't a male prerogative. An entry in Sir Charles's journal in 1825 read, "Widow McHardy denies whisky-brewing, muir-burning and poaching for herself and sons". These were the three great sins in the eyes of the lairds. When their tenants were muir-burning (burning the heather) around their holdings, some of them reclaimed more land than the laird required so that they themselves could cultivate it.

Poaching was also rife (it was in Glen Nochty that one of the North-east's most notorious poachers, Alexander Davidson, was found dead), but whisky-brewing was the most popular way of making a little money on the side. John Milne, a Deeside shoemaker who married a Glenlivet woman and moved to the area, dabbled in it himself. His "Nochty Glens" ran to thirty-seven verses, which he said he composed between breakfast and dinnertime. It told of clashes with the gaugers on Deeside, in the Cabrach and Glen Carry (Glen Carvie), and over Culblean into Cromar. "Burn no more bothies in Mount Sack," it warned the Excisemen.

Mount Sack was Socach, a hill which takes its name from the Gaelic *soc*, meaning the snouty hill. There are two hills called Socach in the Strathdon area, one near Glenbuchat and the other south of the Water of Nochty. Milne's poem, which had a touch of McGonagall about it, showed that although the "highland lads" hated the Excise, they held no grudge against the King whose laws the gaugers were enforcing. The final verse of "Nochty Glens" reads:

> May George IV the crown long wear,
> May all his enemies disappear,
> And his loyal subjects his heart cheer,
> Among Britain's Isles in the morning.

Milne hoped that "the Hanoverian race" would long fill the throne, but the attitude of Geordie's loyal subjects in Strathdon may have had something to do with the fact that the King himself was partial to a drop of Glenlivet, illicit or not.

Aldachuie means the burn of the rain or mist, and it lived up to its name as I climbed away from Duff's Defiance and into the Ladder Hills. This empty landscape, scowling under forbidding rain clouds, is vast and unwelcoming. The track was one of the main droving routes through the Ladder Hills from Glenlivet to Glen Nochty, as well as the road taken by whisky smugglers on their way south. The Ladder, or Ledder, as it was pronounced, is the steep descent on the north side. The Gaelic *monaidhean fharaidh*, ladder hills, is from *faradh*, a ladder – "*Monagan Ary* or ye mountains of ye ladder" was how Gordon's map put it. Another track used by the smugglers, but now scarcely visible, ran from the Well of Lecht to the Braes of Glenlivet.

The main public route north was by the Lecht itself, over the military highway cut out of the harsh hill land by General Wade's successor, General Caulfield. Today, at Allargue, the old pass catapults its travellers out of the Don Valley, zig-zags through two sharp bends, and pitches nervous drivers into a huge lay-by, where they can draw breath before braving the rest of the switchback run. It also serves as a spectacular viewpoint from which passing motorists can enjoy a bird's-eye view of Upper Donside. Below lies Corgarff Castle, stark and white in the green bowl of the valley. It was garrisoned until 1831 as a watchpost against whisky smugglers and was eventually restored by Sir Edmund Stockdale of Delnadamph, along with the Department of the Environment.

Delnadamph, less than a mile away, was bought by the Queen for Prince Charles, who seldom, if ever, stays there, although he shoots over the estate. When the Prince is out with the guns, official-looking cars take up watching positions in the lay-by. In recent years, security has thrown a wide net over these Royal acres.

Three miles on is Britain's highest coffee house. That, at any rate, is what the notices at the Lecht Ski Centre say, although there are probably loftier claims to the title. Jim McIntosh who runs the ski centre with Pieter du Pon, a Dutch-born helicopter pilot, lives in a house that is even higher, bringing up his family – 10-year-old Louise, 7-year-old Nicholas and 3-year-old Annette – in a kind of perpetual winter wonderland. His parents had the post office at Bellabeg, where his father was postmaster.

The ski centre opened twelve years ago. On a good weekend it draws over 2,000 people to the Lecht, including an overspill from the ski slopes at Cairnwell and Cairngorm. The ski-ing development has prodded the authorities into making more strenuous efforts to keep the Lecht open, but there are times when the centre is closed, not because the road is blocked, but simply because conditions are too bad for the public. In 1989, the Lecht's own Devil's Elbow was removed. Here, at a spot called the Double Bends, it took only an inch of snow to make the road impassable. Drivers lost their speed, spun to a halt, and were unable to get their vehicles moving again.

The road plunges down from the ski centre to the Well of Lecht. There is a roadside stone at the well which reads, "AD 1754. Five companies of the 33rd Regiment Right Honourable Lord Charles Hay Colonel made the road from here to the Spey." They could never have dreamed that they were carving out a route for future generations of tourists. One of the first was Queen Victoria, who, lost in Royal wonder at the dour grandeur of the hills, rode through Deeside and Donside on the backs of ponies with

Delnadamph, bought by Her Majesty the Queen for Prince Charles, who shoots over the estate here.

names like Sultan, Fyvie and Lochnagar. On one occasion, avoiding the Lecht on her way home from Tomintoul, she went down to Deeside by Delnabo and Delavorar, following the River Avon to Inchrory and Loch Builg, where a carriage was waiting to take her back to Balmoral. Names like Delnabo and Delavorar throw out sonorous echoes of the days when "loose and broken men" rampaged through these hills.

From the fifteenth to the eighteenth centuries the upper reaches of the River Avon provided a route for traffic in booty from Banffshire and Aberdeenshire to Lochaber and Speyside. A number of military garrisons were set up to combat this pillaging. Corgarff was one of the principal outposts, while another was established at Inchrory. Now, the only shots fired are from the guns of sportsmen stalking over the vast acres of Glenavon deer forest, stretching south and west from Tomintoul. The Glenavon estate, which has more ground over 3,500 ft than any other deer forest in Scotland, includes extensive grouse moors. The average yearly "bag" on the moors totals more than 1,400 brace.

Tomintoul made a poor impression on Queen Victoria. She said it was "the most tumble-down, poor-looking place I ever saw – a long street with three inns, miserably dirty looking houses and people, and a sad look of wretchedness about it". Grant, her head-keeper, added fuel to the fire by saying that it was the dirtiest, poorest village in the whole of the Highlands.

Tomintoul has spent more than a century trying to shrug off that Royal slur. It hasn't completely succeeded, for it is still to some extent a higgledy-piggledy sort of place. From the south, the entrance to the main street is a narrow road that is totally incapable of coping with today's traffic. The old military road has been bypassed just outside the town, so that motorists are now faced with a kind of double dogleg before reaching Queen Victoria's "long street". There is a strong argument for restoring the former military road as the main approach to the town from the south.

The "Town at Tamantoul" may not have reached the glorious heights dreamed of by Alexander, 4th Duke of Gordon, when he planned it in 1776, rashly forecasting that it would soon be "the most populous place in the country", but it has done well for itself. I never counted the hotels and guest houses, but there are certainly more than the three inns noted by Queen Victoria. The Duke of Gordon's instruction that there should be a "right Publick house for the accommodation of Travillers" has been well heeded, which is not surprising in an area where the air is heavy with the smell of peat smoke and whisky.

The Duke also wanted an "unexhaustible moss". He got what he wanted. About two miles north of Tomintoul, on the Dufftown road, a desert of peat stretches west as far as the eye can see. This is Feith Musach (*feith* means a moss or bog), which has been yielding peat to Tomintoul folk since the Duke's planned village first began to take shape.

Whether or not it is inexhaustible is difficult to determine, but it will be a long time before the last peat is cut on the Musach bog. Edward Stuart, who runs a peat-cutting business at Musach (half goes for fuel, half for the whisky maltings), hazards a guess that it is down to about a quarter of the original deposit – and it has taken them two centuries to get there. He has forty-five acres of the moss. He began his one-man operation at Musach in 1983, using a tractor-drawn mechanical cutter, and in his first year produced 5,000 bags of peat, each weighing about half a hundredweight.

Like many other things in this uncompromising North-east landscape, progress depends on the weather. The '80s produced a crop of bad years – '85 was a wet summer, '86 was better (Mr Stuart took out 8,000 bags that year), '87 was almost a disaster ("Just a few tons for the maltings"), '88 showed an improvement, and '89 was good, yielding 1,000 tons. Feith Musach is the biggest peat moss in the area; the nearest of any size is at Nethybridge. Over on the Braes of Glenlivet, where Mr Stuart's father had a farm, there is also a lot of peat, but no moss the size of Musach.

There was a time when people not only cast their own supply of peat, but threw in a few extra loads to sell in the towns. The well-off got others to do the job. In 1750 a labourer was paid 5d a day for casting and by 1790 this had gone up to 10d a day. Leap forward to 1900 and the figure had risen to 1s 6d a day, and by 1950 the distilleries were paying £1 for an eight-hour day.

When Edward Stuart started his operation seven years ago it was unusual to find someone turning the peat on Musach. "Folk were better off and could afford coal," he said. "They had stopped going to the moss." He remembers one year when he saw a lone figure cutting peats there; next year there was none.

Peat is as much a part of Tomintoul's tradition as whisky and grouse. If you want proof of that, go into the museum in the Square, where the first thing you see is a peat cart loaded up as if it had just come from the Musach moss. There is also a display on peat cutting, with tools, photographs and diagrams. Next door is the reconstructed village smiddy, where they once hammered out peat spades on their forges.

Feith Musach will itself become a living museum. Like many other people in Tomintoul, Edward Stuart is gearing himself for the tourist industry. He told me he was planning to open a Reception Centre, where visitors would be able to see for themselves what went on at Musach, both past and present. I hope there is a peat fire in it, for there is nothing quite like the smell of peat smoke; it is redolent of friendly company, good conversation and the pleasures of a dram – the *real* Glenlivet, perhaps. At any rate, it drew me, sniffing the air, beyond the endless brown acres of the Feith Musach to the beckoning Braes of Glenlivet.

CHAPTER 3

ROOSTER'S RIM

T HE BOCHEL IS A PLUM-PUDDING HILL standing guard on the Braes of Glenlivet near the Pole Inn at Knockandhu, on the road from Tomintoul to Dufftown. No one knows how the inn got its name. Jack Shewan, mine host at the Pole, has been there for thirty-two years and still hasn't found an explanation. His own view is that it has a Gaelic origin, particularly since it was an old droving inn. It may have come from *pol*, meaning a pool, but another theory is that the name indicated a crossroads. It is interesting that there is a junction at Auchlossan on Deeside known as the Pole, while a Pole Road branches off the Banff road near Turriff.

Whatever the explanation, there *is* a junction at Knockandhu. Here, a narrow, twisting road runs past the Bochel to the Chapeltown of Glenlivet. In the old days the drovers took their cattle up this track to the Clash of Scalan, from where they went over the hills to the Lecht and Strathdon. Now it is a dead end, a road to nowhere; or, at any rate, nowhere that anybody would want to go. There is nothing but a small distillery, a derelict school, ruined crofts and the dreary prospect of the Ladder Hills. Look at a map and the word "ruin" is everywhere . . . Larryvarry, ruin, Auchavaich, ruin, the Crofts of Scalan, ruin.

The Gaelic word for Scalan is *sgalan*, which was the name given to the turf-roofed sheilings or shelters built for the summer grazings. The remains of these bothies can still be seen scattered about the Glenlivet uplands. The Crofts of Scalan may have gone, but up a dusty dirt-road beyond Chapeltown is the College of Scalan. Looking at it across the Crombie burn, it seems shabby and neglected, ill at ease with the grand title of "College", yet this eighteenth century stone house in the Braes of Glenlivet played an important part in the history of the Catholic Church in Scotland. Founded in 1717 as a Catholic seminary, it trained almost a hundred priests in the eighty years of its existence.

The first of the "heather priests" were taught there, although the original building was burned to the ground by Cumberland's Redcoats after Culloden. Even in this remote corner of Banffshire, Scalan was never free from persecution. It was raided by Hanoverian troops in 1726 and again in 1728. It fell into disrepair in the middle of last century and was used as a barn by a local farmer. Later, it became a dwelling-house, and in more recent years the land was divided into two farms. Seventy-three-year-old Sandy

Sandy Matheson stands beside the old house at Scalan, which in the eighteenth century served as a Catholic seminary, training almost one hundred priests during the eighty years of its existence.

Matheson farmed one of them and now, in his retirement, lives beside the old house.

He showed me through the house, just as he does when he acts as unofficial guide to the visitors who bump up the rough road to Scalan in their cars – and sometimes in busloads – many of them priests, some from as far away as America. The Scalan Association, founded after the war to keep the house in reasonable repair, has done its best, and has at least prevented it from crumbling away like so many other buildings in the area, but it has a sad look about it.

Inside, it is bare and cold, as if life had slowly seeped out of the building. The large room to the right of the entrance is where the boys studied, prayed and ate – *mens sana in corpore sano* (prayer, study, fresh air and exercise) – was their guiding principle – but the big open fireplace offers no warmth or comfort now. Upstairs, recesses that once held box beds gape emptily into the boys' dormitory, and on the second floor there is a tiny chapel where Bishop George Hay, a notable figure in Scalan's history, was consecrated in 1769. When he was a lad of sixteen, he tended Jacobite wounded after the '45 Rising, and, imprisoned for this "crime", was converted to the Catholic faith.

Outside, the Crombie burn gurgles on its way as it did when the Scalan students rose at six o'clock in the morning and washed in its icy waters. Then they ate their spartan breakfast of porridge and got down to work, finishing their day with supper. Inevitably, the last meal of the day was porridge again. The Scalan era ended in 1799, when the seminary was closed and a new college was purchased at Aquhorties, near Inverurie. Later, Aquhorties was succeeded by Blairs, which in turn has now closed.

Before I left Scalan, Sandy Matheson gave my wife a wild rose from the seminary garden. Long after we had gone its scent lingered on, a soft, gentle breath of the past. I was heading for harsher terrain, north to the Blackwater Forest and the Cabrach, where three great glens nudge each other – Glenlivet, Glen Fiddich and Glen Rinnes. This great land mass, scarred by ancient hill tracks and boasting names like Thiefsbush Hill, Thunderclap Hill and Dead Wife's Hillock, stretches from Strathdon to Dufftown.

The lines of a song by George Gordon, an eighteenth-century Cabrach fiddler, were in my mind. It was said that Gordon always sang them before setting out for home after an evening with friends:

> The night it is dark,
> And I canna weel see,
> And wha' will gang through
> The Blackwater wi' me?

When you stand on the stone-hard dome of the Buck of Cabrach and watch the "black weet" sweep across the Blackwater hills, you know that they can be as unpredictable and unfriendly as any of the giant peaks to the west. The "black weet" was what they called rain; black to show it was rain and not "white weet" – snow.

The names on the Ordnance Survey map tell their own story – Powneed, the pool of the nest, a swampy place near Bracklach; Gauch, the windy place; the Roch Ford, where a track from Glenbuchat skirts Creag an Sgor and crosses the Allt Deveron on its way to the Kirktown of Cabrach; and Scad Hill, a bare, scabbed hill that nudges the Buck itself. Nearby is Clayhooter Hill, from the word hooter or hotter, "a quaking, moving mass", a thought which holds no comfort for those who walk the peaty Cabrach braes.

Of all these names, there is one that testifies to the spirit of the people who struggled to make a living from these desolate acres – Reekimlane. It stands near Gauch, off the Glenbuchat-Cabrach track, a modern building now and little like the rough cottar house whose "lum" became a symbol of dogged endurance during the "ill years" of the late eighteenth century. During that famine-stricken time, they hung on in the Cabrach until everything had gone – grain, vegetables, roots and stocks, and then they left. Only one family remained, living on trout caught in the burns, and theirs was the only "reeking lum" to be seen in the district.

Life in the shadow of the Buck was far from easy and it was summed up, a little cruelly, in a rhyme said to have been written by a minister of the parish:

> They ca' the land Cabrach,
> They ca' the people dabrach,
> They ca' the water rooshtair,
> They ca' the corn trooshtair.

Dabrach is the Gaelic *diobarach*, meaning outcast, and trooshtair is *trus-dur*, meaning filth or dirt. The Allt Deveron was known locally as "the Rooshter", from *Ruadh-struth*, the red stream. It was said that the colour of the Deveron water was red, while the Blackwater was black.

"Nothing but hills, hills, hills and hills," wrote one writer, J. G. Philips, who came over to the Cabrach from the Braes of Glenlivet more than a century ago. "There is no bold, rugged outline that makes a mountain grand; no rocks, no precipices, no yawning abysses to make one shrink with horror from the dreadful brink, no foaming and roaring cataracts to excite the imagination and kindle a love for the wild and beautiful, but only a barren desert, where no creature lives, save the red deer of the mountain."

In the kind of land he depicted it would have been easy to believe in creatures like Maggie Molloch, one of the last of the brownies, "a little hairy creatur, in shape of a female child", who had the gift of second sight. It was always the dark side that she saw and when frightened cottars heard her wailing and crying they knew that war and destruction were not far off.

Hairy Meg, as they called her, lived at Auchnarrow, just to the south of Knockandhu, and must have seen the cateran ride past on their way over the old Steplar pass, following a route set out in a 1750 report as "from Achnascra (Achnascraw, near Chapeltown) to Tornachalt (Torniechelt, north of the Kirktown of Cabrach) in the Cabroch by the Sewea (Suie) over the Stepler, a large Mountain, to Blackwater".

She would also have seen signs that told of blood-letting on Carn a' Bhodaich, for it was on the slopes of this hill, on the right bank of the Allt a' Choileachain, that the Battle of Glenlivet was fought on October 3, 1594, between 1200 men led by the Catholic Earls of Huntly and Erroll and a force ten times as strong under the young Earl of Argyll. One of those who lost his life in the battle was Sir Patrick Gordon of Auchindoun.

The fifteenth-century castle of Auchindoun, a Gordon stronghold overlooking the Fiddich, stood sentinel on the hill road from Dufftown to the Cabrach and Donside before it was burned down by a raiding party of Mackintoshes in 1592:

> Coming owre Cairn Croom
> And looking doun, man,
> I saw Willie Macintosh
> Burn Auchindoun, man.

Mary Queen of Scots, turning up her nose at the rebellious Gordons, deliberately passed

Glen Fiddich, a former haunt of Queen Victoria. The green hills that she described in her *Journal* are now under massive afforestation.

by Auchindoun in 1564, but in 1867 Queen Victoria had a look at the castle ruins on her way to Glenfiddich Lodge. Another Royal traveller, Edward I, came this way in 1296 when he marched south from Elgin, going "over the mountaynes" of the Cabrach to Kildrummy. "The Mundaie he wente into Interkeratche," wrote a contemporary chronicler. "Interkeratche" was Inverharroch, now a farm on the road to Dufftown.

When I went down Glen Fiddich, following in Queen Victoria's footsteps, I had her *Journal* to guide me – "Here you go quite into the hills. The glen is very narrow, with the Fiddich flowing below, green hills rising on either side with birch trees growing on them. We saw deer on the tops of the hills close by. The carriage-road – a very good one – winds along for nearly three miles, when you come suddenly upon the lodge." Not much has changed since the Queen wrote that, except that the green hills are now under massive afforestation.

The lodge gates were locked when I entered the glen, and I thought I would be met by an irate keeper demanding to know why I was trespassing. I half-expected the lodge to have a Victorian air about it, some link with the days when elegant carriages sat outside and guests strolled in the grounds or held picnics on the riverbank. From some distance away, the building – "a long shooting lodge, but only one story high" – looked impressive. When I drew near it I became uneasily aware that the track ran right past the front door.

But there was nobody there, no carriages, no cars, no people, no sign of life, and the picture I had in my mind of this stately Highland home quickly disintegrated. A sign pointed to the front door, but there no longer was a front door; or, at any rate, only part of one, standing open, half of it rotting away, some of it missing. Inside, paint peeled from the ceilings and the huge kitchen was empty. The whole place had an air of neglect and decay. Estate workers' houses were abandoned, windows broken, rooms deserted. It was hard to believe that the old Queen had ever stayed there. These old lodges encapsulate a little piece of history, and I will never be able to understand why they are allowed to fall into rack and ruin.

For me, the history of Glen Fiddich became a kind of jigsaw to be pieced together. Looking along the passage that ran from the hall to the end of the building, I began to fit the Royal entourage into their rooms, using Victoria's *Journal*: "Sir Thomas Biddulph's room, then the Duke's, then Brown's and Ross's (in one), then, Louise's, then mine, then Emilie's and Annie's (in one), then a little further back, Jane Churchill's and her maid's – all very comfortable and conveniently together."

The Queen was unhappy on that first night at Glen Fiddich. Her luggage was held up at Dufftown and she had no clothes to wear, not even a "nightie". She sat waiting for her luggage to appear, growing increasingly irritated, disliking "the idea of going to bed without any of the necessary toilette". A man was sent out with a lantern to look for the missing cart, but there was no sign of it. It turned up at half-past four in the morning, but the Queen, exhausted, had made "some arrangements which were very uncomfortable" and had gone to bed.

So I left the old lodge and its memories and went on up the track. There was some life in the glen; two dogs howled at me from kennels across the river, but I turned uphill, away from the Fiddich. Below me, on the left, was the burn where a cave called the Elf House burrows its way under the heather – the *Cave Elf House*, according to the O.S. map. The Duke of Richmond told Queen Victoria that it went a long way under the hill. From the Elf House, Victoria rode across the moors by what she called "the Sowie" (Suie), going over the Steplar until she came to Carn na Bruar and looked down the Livet towards Tomnavoulin.

I wonder if they told her about James an Tuam – James of the Hill. This notorious freebooter was in an Edinburgh jail when he saw a man called Grant of Tomnavoulin passing under his window. "What news from Speyside?" he shouted. "None very particular" replied the Tomnavoulin man. "The best is that the country is rid of you." 'Perhaps we'll meet again,' said James. Later, the outlaw escaped and headed north to Speyside. He called at Tomnavoulin, slew Grant and his son, and after cutting off their heads threw the bloody trophies into Mrs Grant's lap.

The old track that Queen Victoria followed after leaving the Elf's House would have taken her out at Tomnavoulin. The path I was on climbed up Corryhabbie Hill, where Morton's Way runs south and both the Fiddich and Livet have their source. From there I could see across to Tomnavoulin and north to Dufftown and Ben Rinnes. The writer Lachlan Shaw said that James an Tuam (his real name was James Grant of Carron) hid in a cave on top of Ben Rinnes.

The day I climbed Ben Rinnes a fierce wind was blustering in from the east, snapping around the rocks and shrieking off down the Burn of Lyneirach to where it joins the River Avon. There were eerie cadences in its endless sough. Near here, where the Avon meets the Spey, is the Cow Haugh and in this lovely setting stands Ballindalloch Castle. When it was built in 1546 by Patrick, the first of the Grants of Ballindalloch, the laird planned to build it higher up, but when the walls began to rise a great wind came whirling down from Ben Rinnes, blowing the stones into the river and the master and his man into a holly tree.

What happened after that, according to the storytellers, was that a ghostly laugh sounded out and an eldritch voice cried three times, 'Build in the cow haugh!' So there it was built and there it remains, and maybe the smell of sulphur still hangs over the holly tree where the laird of Ballindalloch was couped all those years ago by the De'il, for it was his knoll that was marked out for the original site.

Here, in this wild country, there are ruined crofter cottages all around. I remember a farmer at Aldunie in the Cabrach telling me that the empty cottages in that area were all occupied in 1947. Twenty families moved out in the thirty years after that. It was also said that every house had its private still; in one year the names of eighty people were recorded as having engaged in illicit distilling in the Upper Cabrach. Not all that long ago they were still recalling a Cabrach man who, in a panic, hid his 'pottie' in a hole at the burnside and was never able to find it again.

When I went down into Glen Rinnes from Corryhabbie I passed the spot – the Folds of Corryhabbie – where Robbie Macpherson, a well-known Glen Rinnes whisky smuggler, had his 'brew pot'. He would have kept one eye on Meikle Conval, flanking Ben Rinnes, for it was up there that the folk of Dufftown used to light fires to warn illicit whisky-makers that the Excisemen had just passed through the town.

The old tag says that if Rome was built on seven hills, Dufftown was built on seven stills, but the number has long since become outdated. Nevertheless, there are seven distilleries within walking distance of the centre of the town. Six of them belong to last century: Mortlach, going back to 1823, Convalmore (1869), Glenfiddich (1866), Balvenie (1892), Dufftown (1896), and Glendullan (1897). The seventh is Pittyvaich, which went into operation in 1974.

The name Pittyvaich stirs other memories. Mary Symon, the poet, lived there. A friend of Hugh MacDiarmid's, she made a name for herself with her poems lamenting the dead of the 1914-18 war and when her first volume was published in 1933 it was sold out in a week. She died at Pittyvaich in 1938. Sadly, she is not well remembered. Her poems belong to another age, to a now almost-forgotten war, but they should be treasured for the picture they paint of a way of life long since lost to these northern glens. Her description of a roup (sale) in January, 1918, is worth preserving:

> They cam' wi' stirks, they cam' wi' strae,
> They cam' wi' horse an' hen;
> The road wis black wi' booin' back
> Near hauf-wye up the Glen.

There were gigs, prams and flauchter-spades, canty wives with scones and butter-pats, and 'a ruck o' aul' lum hats', reminding onlookers of the day the saddler lent *his* lum hat to Auchnagyle and it came back 'like a concertina in a cloot'. There were bowlies, teapots, plates and juggies, one of which went to Skinflint Tam for a threepenny bit, and by the time the roup was finished there was nothing left but 'twa mismarrowed sheen'.

Mary Symon's thoughts were never very far from the war that emptied the glen of its menfolk. The roup [sale] that she wrote about was held to send money to the 'sodger lads', and all its fun and laughter died in the knowledge that some of them might not 'hear the whaup on the hills again'. It was to the hills that she turned when she longed for the return of her sodger loons and grieved for the ones who would not come back. Their remembrance was a 'lanely cairn on a hameland hill'.

> Doon, laich doon, the Dullan sings,
> An' I ken o' an aul' sauch [willow] tree,
> Where a wee loon's wahnie's [rod] hingin' yet
> That's dead in Picardy.

Queen Victoria followed the Dullan on her way to Glenfiddich. She recorded in her *Journal* how she entered Glen Livet through Knockandhu, 'just behind the celebrated Glenlivet Distillery'. Later, after going into Glen Rinnes, the Royal party stopped to have tea at a spot where there was 'a very pretty view of Glenlivet'. It is an odd thing that Glenlivet the whisky – 'the celebrated Glenlivet' – is better known than Glenlivet the place.

Glenlivet was bought by the Crown Estate in 1937, but since then it has been largely left to its own devices. It covers some 60,000 acres, much of it farming country (there are forty let farms on the estate), but also takes in forestry and sporting interests – grouse moors, salmon fishings and deerstalking. The Cromdale and Ladder hills carry large stocks of red grouse, attracting an international clientèle to Glenlivet in August and September. This, along with deerstalking and salmon fishing, maintains a tradition going back to the days of the Dukes of Gordon.

Forestry is comparatively new to Glenlivet. The pine and spruce woods cloaking the hills were planted in the 1950s and extend to 8500 acres. The planting was done in consultation with the farming tenants. The Crown's main concern in the past has been to look after its tenants, but recently it has been taking a more general interest in the economic welfare of the area, as well as that of the 'Town of Tamantoul', which is part of the estate.

Neil Sutherland, the Glenlivet estate development manager, was seconded from the Highlands and Islands Development Board to look at possible new enterprises and activities. If they are to develop the economy of the area, he says, they have to look seriously at tourism, but they also have to keep in mind that it is primarily a farming area. It has to be compatible with that.

His main aim is to put Glenlivet on the map; not the whisky (it's already there), but the place. He is well aware that when most people hear the name Glenlivet they think only of malt whisky. He admits that when he moved to Tomintoul he had heard of the whisky, but knew very little about the place. Now he is out to give it an identity.

Neil hopes that inexperienced walkers will stay away from the more remote areas. Although unwilling to encourage the uninitiated to go wandering in the wilderness on their own, he hopes that some visitors will be able to 'gang through the Blackwater' with a ranger.

When you wander among the 'heather and whaups, and whins and mist' in this wild land it is best to think of the King of the Cabrach, whose realm spread from the 'Rooster' north across the moors to Balloch. Of course, he wasn't a *real* King, not like the ones who go riding about the glens on their fancy ponies. All he had was a 'sheltie' and a wheezing old dog at his side. Yet he was still 'a gey bit kingie', according to Mary Symon in her poem 'The Hedonist'. He had his values and his priorities in place:

> Weel-suppered an' slockit [quenched], they'd saddle him
> On a shalt's as sweers himsel',
> An' he'd ride his realm fae the Rooster's rim
> To the lythe [shelter] o' the Balloch well;
> An' his bodygaird was a fozelin' tyke [wheezing dog]
> As ready to row's to run –
> 'I'm a king,' says he, 'I can dae as I like
> An' I'm giein' my fowk their fun.'

As Mary Symon said, he had no soul, no siller [money] and no sense, but he did fine without all three. He had a drouth [thirst] that could drink the Deveron dry and he would argue that the more good you put into his mouth, the more came out. He wanted his epitaph to read: 'He garts a' laugh'. It was a simple enough philosophy – if you can make people laugh, there can't be much wrong with you.

CHAPTER 4

WHISKY GLENS

W HATEVER GEORGE IV THOUGHT OF HIS SCOTTISH SUBJECTS he had a soft spot in his heart – and his palate – for their whisky. During the Royal visit in 1822, John Grant of Rothiemurchus wrote to his wife from Edinburgh telling her that the King drank nothing but whisky. He was, said Grant, "an admirable judge of glen livat". The Laird of Rothiemurchus was in the running for a judge's post in India, and, with his eye on the main chance, asked his wife to send on "a dozen of our best". He added, "Eliza knows where to find it".

Eliza was Elizabeth Grant, who was to become well-known for her *Memoirs of a Highland Lady*. In the book she told how, after Lord Conyngham, husband of the King's mistress, had searched everywhere for pure Glenlivet whisky, her father sent word to her to empty her "pet bin", where there was "whisky long in the wood, long in uncorked bottles, mild as milk, and the true contraband *gout* in it". The whisky, along with fifty brace of ptarmigan, was sent off to Holyrood House. Elizabeth grudged sending "this treasure" to the King, but admitted that it "made our fortunes" – her father got his job in India.

Royal Geordie's liking for Glenlivet must have given a considerable boost to its popularity (the Royal link is still plugged by its makers today) and in the years that followed more and more distilleries began to cash in on the name. At one time there were twenty-eight distilleries using it in one way or another, so that Glenlivet was known sarcastically as the longest glen in Scotland. In the end a court decision ruled that only the Minmore distillery could call itself *The* Glenlivet, but many distilleries got over the problem by hyphenating their name with the Livet tag – *Glenforres-Glenlivet*, *Tamnavoulin-Glenlivet*, and so on. Some still do.

It is difficult to pinpoint what gives *The Glenlivet* its special flavour. Some people say that the water's the thing; after all, the Gaelic *uisge beatha* means the water of life. Sir Robert Bruce Lockhart, whose great-grandfather founded Balmenach Distillery in Cromdale, said that "pure Highland water" gave Scotch whisky its special excellence. The water for Glenlivet whisky comes from Josie's Well, but nobody seems to know who Josie was, so if he knew the secret it died with him.

Wullie Gray at Corgarff on Donside, whose sheep farm borders the Braes of

Glenlivet, would probably argue that the water on his farm at the Luib is as good as anything that Josie produced. He unearthed a spring on the Luib which he thinks gives the clearest, purest water you could find anywhere. He gave me a glass of it, ice-cold and refreshing, and then he poured me a generous dram of Glenfiddich and said, "See what it does to the whisky". I don't know what it did to the whisky, but it tasted like nectar – as mild as milk.

One visitor to the Luib, Mrs Nora Coutts, from Swindon, a native of the North-east, was so impressed by the water that she played Wullie at his own game and wrote a poem about it, calling it 'Wullie's Watter':

> 'Twas clear as crystal, diamon' bricht
> An' trickl't ower ma lips,
> It was a better drink by far
> Than a' yer Hielan' nips.

Wullie replied in kind, with the result that a poetic correspondence has flowed between Swindon and Corgarff ever since. Wullie hoped that Nora would return to the Luib, adding:

> So fan ye come, jist ca' in by,
> We'd love tae hear ye sing,
> An' ye can hae yer fill, my lass,
> O' watter fae the Spring.

> An' as ye sip yer watter clear
> I hope yer man an' me
> Will match yer ilka glaiss for glaiss,
> Thinned doon wi' barley bree.

Wullie didn't say whether the water would be "thinned doon" with Glenlivet or Glenfiddich. The two are said to run neck and neck in the whisky stakes. As we sat by his fireside at the Luib, Wullie, with his stockinged feet up on the Raeburn, sipped his Glenfiddich and offered a taste of it to his pet hen, Goldie, who pecked at it with considerable relish. Goldie, incidentally, got her name because she snatched a gold earring from Mrs Gray's ear and swallowed it.

There isn't a distillery at Corgarff, so the water from Wullie's spring will never be used to make a new brand of Luib whisky. The nearest they get to that these days is a mock still on display at Corgarff Castle, from which, ironically, soldiers once hunted the whisky smugglers. Over on Deeside, another mock still can be seen at the Royal Lochnagar Distillery, where Queen Victoria and Prince Albert sampled the local brew in 1845. Whisky by the gallon was delivered in casks to Balmoral Castle, where, according to reports, the drinking that went on among the staff had to be seen to be believed.

Balmoral had its share of illicit stills (there were a dozen "black bothies" in nearby Glen Girnock), but every glen you go into has its stories about whisky smuggling. The chances of finding a real whisky bothy, or even the remains of one, are remote. Minmore, home of *The Glenlivet*, has on display a large-scale reproduction of Landseer's painting, *Highland Whisky Still*. Landseer said there were "lots of whisky stills to be found" when he did this painting in 1829, but, although it was a great success at the Royal Academy, it seems to me to be an exaggerated version of the real thing.

Long before *The Glenlivet* was given its exclusive prefix, the whisky was known as *Smith's Glenlivet*. Smith – George Smith – was the founder of the Glenlivet distillery. A former whisky smuggler, he realised that the 1823 Act of Parliament legalising distilling would put an end to his "black bothy" trade, so he took out a licence to distil on his farm at Upper Drumin in 1824. In 1859 he opened the present distillery at Minmore, and in 1875 the company registered "The Glenlivet" as its trade mark.

Today, over a century and a half later, thousands of visitors flock to Minmore to see how the *real* Glenlivet is made. The statistics are staggering. Here, they turn out 5.2 million litres of whisky a year – 250 million bottles – and there are 57,000 casks in the Minmore warehouses. It is a sobering thought that the whisky visitors see being made in Glenlivet at present will not be drunk until next century. I was told about one special bottle stored away at Minmore – a malt marking the wedding of Prince Charles and Diana. The cost – £150.

'Balmenach, Craggan, an' Minmore' were mentioned in Scott Skinner's famous strathspey, 'The Glenlivet'. Balmenach is one of 127 malt distilleries clustered about the Spey and the Livet, running south from Elgin to the Braes of Glenlivet. Alfred Barnard visited it while on the epic tour which led to the publication of his book, *The Whisky Distilleries of the United Kingdom* in 1887.

Barnard reached it by going up the Cromdale Burn, where he saw a range of hills – the Cromdales – in front of him. It was over this range that I made my way to Balmenach, following the route taken by James Macgregor, who founded the distillery, when he crossed the hills from Tomintoul to start a new life in Cromdale with his two brothers. .

It isn't clear why the Macgregors left Tomintoul, for it was a lively enough place. In 1794 the *Statistical Account of Scotland* said of the folk in Tomintoul, "All of them sell whisky and all of them drink it," adding, "When disengaged from this business, the women spin yarns, kiss their inamorattas, or dance to the discordant strains of an old fiddle". Perhaps Tomintoul was too lively for the Macgregors, or perhaps the gaugers were hot on their heels.

In Cromdale, one of the brothers started a mill, another went into a farm at the Mains of Cromdale, and the third, James, took a farm at Balmenach, augmenting his income with a spot of illicit distilling. An excise officer who came to inspect the farm showed an interest in a rough stone building with a mill-wheel and a mill-lade. When he asked what it was he was told it was a peat shed. Before he left, warmed by a dram from James's bottle, he said quietly: "If I were you, Mr Macgregor, I'd just take out a licence for yon peat shed". The hint was taken – and, in 1824, Balmenach distillery came into being.

Up on the Cromdale hills I paused at a huge cairn built on the spot where a bonfire was lit to mark the Coronation of King Edward VII in 1902. Away to the north lay the moors of Tulchan, where Edward, when he was Prince of Wales, went grouse-shooting, as did the Duke of York, the future King George V.

From Edward's cairn I looked out over the magnificent view that faced the Macgregor brothers when they first arrived at Balmenach. The hills of Cromdale form a ridge that stretches for some eight miles between the Spey and the Avon, seldom falling below 2000 ft. Cromdale means "crooked plain", a name that takes on some significance when you see the winding Spey from above the haughs. To the south was Craigan a' Chaise (2367 ft), the highest point in the Cromdales, where there is another cairn commemorating Queen Victoria's jubilee in 1887.

Below, spreading out from Claggersnich Wood, was the bleak moorland where English horses had "bath'd their hoofs in Highland blood" three hundred years ago. This was at the Battle of Cromdale, fought in May, 1690, when the remnants of Claverhouse's army were routed by a mixed Anglo-Scottish force. There is a reminder of that mournful day in the ruins of Lethendry Castle, where the Jacobites took shelter after the battle. When I was there, Ian Hay, a local Excise Officer, was planning a re-enactment of the battle to mark its 300th anniversary. There are various versions of it (Montrose gets mixed up with it in one of the ballads) and Ian was trying to decide which account should be used for the 1990 "battle". He also had a problem with uniforms for, as he told me, the Government troops were not Redcoats (which would have made it easy), but were dressed more like Cromwell's Ironsides.

When I made my way downhill I passed the *Clach nam Piobair*, the Piper's Stone, where a Jacobite piper is said to have made his last stand. It is an unimpressive memorial; a plain stone wedged against a tree on the edge of Claggersnich Wood. The folk of Cromdale would do well to erect another cairn on top of the hill to commemorate the battle.

But I was thinking of more peaceful things when I came down to Balmenach . . . of whisky, "a daily necessity", always on the table at Balmenach or in a keg beside the dining-room door, of a youngster playing hide-and-seek on Tom Liath, and of boys with shilling rods and a tin of worms wandering up the Cromdale burn, flushing snipe from the bogs and grouse from the heather, and going home with baskets full of trout.

One of the lads with the shilling rod was Sir Robert Bruce Lockhart, who, in his book, *Scotch*, looked back to the days when he roamed the Cromdale moors "far from the eagle eye of my Macgregor grandmother". Jean Macgregor was said by Sir Robert to be a remarkable woman. Curiously enough, when I was at Balmenach the manager, Ernie Oakes, told me he had had a visit from her great-grandson, John Bruce Lockhart, who lives in East Sussex and was also making a nostalgic trip back to the scenes of his childhood. He described his grandmother as "a formidable, able tyrant who ruled the family with a rod of iron – and half the countryside as well".

But it was the Cromdale burn that John Bruce Lockhart remembered with most affection . . . and the days when he fished this "boys' paradise" in the late 1920s. He told Ernie that when he was a boy the trout in the burn were "whoppers". Of course, the fish are always bigger in the days of your youth, or seem to be; sixty years later, when John Lockhart took up his rod and tried his luck again, they were a good deal smaller.

When Alfred Barnard visited Balmenach, he was shown a double-arched cavern, dug deep into the hill, fifty yards from the distillery. Here, said Barnard, a noted band of smugglers carried on their operations. The gaugers were told about this hide-out by an informer. Armed to the teeth, they crept through the narrow entrance to the cave, but one of the smugglers spotted the Excisemen. He instantly unhooked a pipe connecting the smugglers' furnace with a concealed chimney in the roof and fired his pistol at the gaugers. In the dense smoke from the furnace the smugglers escaped, but the officers destroyed the still and demolished the cave.

The distillery manager took Barnard to another smugglers' bothy, one of the largest in the Glenlivet area, within two hundred yards of the distillery, but Ernie Oakes was unable to do the same. All traces of the smuggling days have gone. It was the same when I went north to Dail-Uaine Distillery at Carron, south of Aberlour, where I half-expected to see some ghostly figures working their illicit still in one of the burns. There was, according to Barnard, "a nest of bold smugglers" at Carron and the ruins of one of their bothies was pointed out to him on the distillery premises.

They say that there was a haunted bothy in a rocky cavern through which one of the Dail-Uaine burns runs. "There," wrote Barnard, "the still-fires are seen weirdly sparkling like eyes of diamonds, and the ghosts of the departed smugglers busy at their ancient avocations. This discovery was made one winter's night by a shepherd, who took shelter in a cleft of the rock from the bleak winds and drifting snow." The shepherd apparently refused to say if he had "tasted the ghostly spirit", and even Barnard thought that a stiff glass of Dail-Uaine might have had something to do with it.

The Haugh of Carron lies in some of the prettiest country on Speyside. Barnard, already captivated by "the enchanting loveliness of Strathspey", thought that the Dailuaine distillery was in "one of the most beautiful little glens in Scotland". His description of the area might have leapt from one of today's tourist brochures – "Never was there such a soft, bright landscape of luxuriant green, of clustering foliage, and verdant banks of wild flowers, ferns and grasses. The whole scene is dainty enough for a fairy's palace."

Dailuaine is a Gaelic name meaning "the green vale" and nothing could be more appropriate, but it is also a name that has become synonymous with whisky. It was given to the distillery by William Mackenzie, a farmer at Carron and Rinnachat, when he set up his still in a hollow by the Carron Burn in 1851. So, all these years later, the smell of peat still tickles your nostrils as you go down the green vale into Carron. At the top of the hill a row of regimented houses runs the length of Dailuaine Terrace; they were distillery workers' houses, but some of them have been sold. There is not much to the village itself, except the Carron Inn, which is only a stone's throw from another distillery, the Imperial.

When I was with Ronnie Grant, the manager of Dailuaine, I noticed a curious lock

Ronnie Grant, the manager of Dailuaine Distillery, holding an implement for sampling whisky. The outsize brass Excise lock behind him now serves as a trophy for a competition, Distillers v Excise.

hanging on the wall of his office. It was an outsize brass Excise lock, which, with a large key to open it, turned out to be a trophy for a competition, Distillers v Excise. Nowadays, it seems, there are only peaceful "battles" between the whisky-makers and the gaugers.

Maybe Barnard's shepherd, cowering among the rocks in the Carron Burn, was speaking the truth, for everywhere you go on the whisky trail you are chasing ghosts. Walk the Cromdale hills, climb Corryhabbie and go down through the Braes of Glenlivet, and you are forever leaping over burns with rickles of stones that might have been whisky bothies.

In the old days, sturdy little garrons carried smugglers' whisky over the hills to markets in the south, but horses were no less important in the legitimate whisky trade. Cart sheds and stables were a familiar part of the distillery scene, and Barnard made frequent reference to the delivery of barley and the transport of whisky by horse and cart. George Smith of Glenlivet kept "numerous teams of magnificent horses", and Barnard said that he "passed as many as sixteen during our drive up to the distillery".

Glenlivet, like many other distilleries, was sited in an out-of-the-way part of the country which, although ideal for whisky smugglers dodging the gaugers, was unsuitable for transporting legitimate whisky to markets in the south. It had to be taken by horse and cart over many miles of difficult country to ports like Garmouth and Burghead on the Moray Firth and then sent south by boat. The coming of the railway made life easier, but even when the Speyside railway was extended to Ballindalloch it still left Glenlivet seven miles from the railhead.

Nevertheless, the use of the railway was a major step forward for the whisky-makers. When Barnard was on his epic tour in 1887, he noted that a tramway was about to be laid at Balmenach, taking whisky to Cromdale station, and that plans were being made for the laying of a tramline at Dailuaine, where the distillery had been connected by telephone to Carron station. Here, however, it took twenty years before the Dailuaine, Imperial and Carron warehouses were linked by sidings to the railhead.

The whisky-men took immense pride in their engines. The first "puffer" to ride the rails at Dailuaine was a saddle-tank locomotive made by Barclay of Kilmarnock in 1897. It worked the line until 1939, when it was replaced by another Barclay engine, Dailuaine No. 1. Twenty years later, a retired British Railways engine driver described No. 1 as "a joy to behold", with well-cleaned paintwork and polished brass and copper. This much-loved distillery pug worked a five-day week, shunting rakes of three or four wagons, until the Strathspey line was condemned in 1967. "Dailuaine" was presented to the Strathspey Railway Company by the Scottish Railway Preservation Society.

The miniature railway at Balmenach, as Barnard had seen, was laid in 1897, when an Aveling Porter geared locomotive was bought to link the distillery with Cromdale station. It was used to shunt filled casks to the exchange sidings and to bring in empty casks, coal and barley for malting. This was replaced in 1936 by a new pug built at Andrew Barclay's Caledonia Works in Kilmarnock. The "Balmenach", as it was called, steamed out of the distillery for the last time on 31 October, 1968, a few days before the Speyside line was finally closed to freight traffic. The engine was presented to the Strathspey Railway Museum at Boat of Garten in 1977.

So now there are only memories of the whisky lines. They fed into the main Strathspey railway, constructed in 1863 as an offshoot of the Great North of Scotland Railway. When it reached Carron, on the opposite side of the Spey, the bridge over the river vastly improved Dailuaine distillery's communications with the outside world. Today, some of the stations have been absorbed into the Speyside Way, the long-distance footpath opened in 1967. Planned to run from the Cairngorms to the sea, it stretches at present from Spey Bay on the Moray Firth to Ballindalloch, with spurs to Dufftown and Tomintoul. The next stage will be an extension from Ballindalloch to Glenmore.

Between Craigellachie and Aberlour the Way takes you through the only tunnel on the Strathspey railway. It passes three distilleries on its way to Ballindalloch – the Imperial at Carron, Knockandhu and Tamdhu. Tamdhu still keeps one foot in the whisky industry, for the former station has been converted into a distillery visitors'

The former Ballindalloch Station, now a feature of the long-distance footpath known as the Speyside Way.

One reaches a pleasant picnic spot at the old Blacksboat Station on the Speyside Way.

centre. Blacksboat, farther south, has become a pleasant picnic spot.

Four miles south of Tamdhu, walkers cross the impressive viaduct that carried the railway over the Spey and come to the end of their tramp along the Speyside Way. Farther south, where the line pushed its way through the Haughs of Cromdale, the old terminus for the Balmenach whisky train is a ghost station. The buildings are boarded up and derelict, and waist-high weeds claw the old station towards extinction.

It seems only yesterday that the whisky trains were running. Ernie Oakes, who is a local man and has been manager at Balmenach for four years, remembers when the mainline whisky train ran from Craigellachie to Aviemore pulling twenty to thirty open-topped railway vans, picking up whisky delivered to the various stations by the distillery pugs. Back in the fifties and sixties they started putting railway police on the bridges because people were jumping into the wagons while the train was going up to Aviemore, helping themselves to whisky and jumping off again with their loot. They were, I imagine, descendants of the men who operated the black bothies in the hills.

Sir Robert Bruce Lockhart said that the greatest thrill he ever had at Balmenach was in climbing into the cab of the pug that ran to Cromdale station. The men who operated these miniature locomotives took tremendous pride in keeping them spotlessly clean, highly polished, and in good working order. Sir Robert made friends with the driver of "Balmenach". He was "a magnificent figure of a man called Long John", who let young Lockhart and his friend instal themselves in the cab and pretend they were driving the engine.

I went to see one of Long John's successors – the man who drove the last Balmenach puggy. Robbie Alanach lives in a cottage at Feabuie, down a rough track that branches off a road to the distillery. Beyond it another track pushes on to Burnside, where the streams come tumbling down from the Cromdale hills. Robbie was having a lunchtime dram when I arrived at Feabuie, but it was rum he was drinking, not whisky. He showed me pictures of his old engine, which he drove up and down the Balmenach–Cromdale line for over ten years. When the line closed, Robbie worked in the warehouse for another ten years before retiring.

We stood outside Feabuie, looking across to where smoke drifted up from the distillery chimney. In the stillness that lay over the Haughs you could almost hear the thin whistle of Robbie's puggy as it grumbled across the moor from Cromdale station. It was always a big push up the hill, he said. From where we stood we could see the dark triangle of Claggersnich Wood and the track climbing up the heather-clad slopes to where the Macgregor brothers had come marching over the hills from Tomintoul so many years ago. I thought of how James Macgregor had built his first still in the lap of these hills. I could imagine him sitting in his tiny office filling in his ledger entry for 18th August, 1824, recording the sale of "10 gallons of aqua 11 over-proof" at 9 shillings per gallon duty-paid to William Milne of Broad Street, Aberdeen.

Later, he had more important clients, among them the Earl of Selkirk and the Duke of Bedford. When Alfred Barnard was at Balmenach he tasted some of their 1873 whisky, the same whisky that was sent to the Gairloch Hotel at Loch Maree in 1878 for another customer who appreciated a good dram. This was Queen Victoria, who "found it prime, and far superior in our opinion to old brandy".

CHAPTER 5

LAND

OF

PEACE

THE BALMENACH ENGINE LAY ABANDONED at the end of the track in Boat of Garten station. Robbie Alanach, angry at the fate of his beloved "pug", had told me that it had been allowed to fall to bits, but the truth was that it had simply been put out to grass, like an old workhorse, along with an assortment of restaurant cars, rail trolleys, sleeping cars, brake vans, tank wagons, a district engineer's saloon and three Victorian carriages. Here, in a station that takes its name from the ferry that once plied across the River Spey, they have created a dream-world for railway buffs and little boys wanting to be engine drivers.

Across the track from the "Balmenach", the Strathspey Railway's steam locomotive No. 2996 was snorting impatiently alongside the main platform, ready to begin its run from Boat of Garten to Aviemore. The vintage hoardings on the station fence advertised Bermaline Bread and Rowntree's chocolates, while another poster urged nervous travellers to consider the terms offered by the Passengers Railway Assurance Company. There used to be one boasting the quality of Spratt's Dog Cakes and Puppy Biscuits, but I must have missed it.

I climbed on board and off we went, puffing our way into the past. There was another reminder of the old whisky trains when we passed a carriage carrying the crest "Glenfiddich – Standfast". It made me think of John Campbell Shairp, poet, critic and Professor of Latin at St. Andrews University, who back in 1864 borrowed the Clan Grant war-cry, "Standfast, Craig-Ellachie", when he wrote a poem casting a mournful eye over the route of the new railway from Perth to Inverness – up through "grisly, storm resounding Badenoch", along the Spey to Rothiemurchus, and past "dark Glen More and cloven Glen Feschie."

Professor Shairp regretted the rape of the "haughty solitudes" and could see little good coming from the iron monsters that rumbled over the Pass of Drumochter to Speyside. "The old charm is disenchanted," he wrote. "The old Highlands are no more."

A cheerful group of workers at Boat of Garten Station on the Strathspey Railway Line in 1980. By courtesy of Aberdeen Journals Ltd.

The passengers on No. 2996 were trying to recapture some of that charm by travelling on the "iron horses" that the Professor had disliked so much. The Strathspey Railway, which was reopened in 1978, has as its armorial bearings an osprey, two gold crowns of the Clan Grant, a locomotive wheel, and a wavy blue line representing the River Spey, and it is an interesting thought that its Gaelic motto, *Ath Bheirte*, means "Re-born".

Professor Shairp wasn't the only one who had misgivings about the coming of the railway. The twin tracks cutting through Shairp's "land of bens and glens and corries" also encroached on the territory that Queen Victoria had made her own, blazing Royal trails by pony and on foot in her Great Expeditions. In 1861, three years before Shairp launched his attack on the railway, one of the Queen's expeditions took her through the Professor's "cloven Glen Feschie" to Dalwhinnie and over the Pass of Drumochter to Blair Atholl. "The railroad will come," she predicted, adding gloomily, "I cannot help regretting it." What she could never have foreseen was that her own love of Scotland would give the railroad its biggest boost, and that twelve years later, travelling in the opposite direction, she would go over the Pass of Drumochter again – by train.

Watching the scenery from the window of No. 2996, I saw the grey outline of the Cairngorms looming up. We rolled over the levelcrossing installed in 1980 for the new road to Dalfaber Village, the time-share development that has helped to swell Aviemore's tourist population, and then, hissing and steaming, pulled to a halt at the station. Across a wire fence separating us from the main line, a sleek inter-city diesel slipped by, heading for Inverness, blowing its whistle in a respectful salute to the age of steam.

Looking across the village I could see four road and rail links running in parallel lines, bringing past and present together. They were the Strathspey line, the British Railways main line, the road through Aviemore to Carrbridge and the north, and the A9 dual carriageway. The old and new motor roads, along with stretches of Wade roads

Mr Alan Devereux, OBE, inaugurating the Aviemore Tourist Complex, covering 130 acres at Dalfaber, in September 1980. By courtesy of Aberdeen Journals Ltd.

built two and a half centuries ago, chase each other all the way south to Dunkeld and Perth. Despite the growth of fast, modern roads the railways have also seen change, so that the Aviemore station has developed rather than diminished in importance in recent years. The increase of through passenger traffic on the Perth–Inverness rail line has led to the reinstatement of passing loops at Kincraig, Slochd and Moy.

The Slochd, near Moy, is the gateway to Speyside from the north. The name Slochd Muic means the Hole of the Pig, or the Lair of the Wild Boar. Today, dramatic though it is as it cuts through a great mass of rock rising on each side of the road, the Slochd Pass is a lot less daunting than it was two or three centuries ago. Then, according to one report, the mountains on either side of the pass were so precipitous that you could see nothing but the heavens above and a hill on either side.

Between Moy and the Slochd summit is Strathdearn, thrusting deep into the Monadhliath mountains. The Spey runs its glittering course between the Cairngorms and the Monadhliaths, but the area to the north is uncharted territory to most of the tourists who flock to Speyside. Conservationists and climbers fret and fume over the future of the Cairngorms, the red mountains, but little thought is given to the Monadhliaths, the grey mountains.

The historian W. Douglas Simpson described them as "this despised mountain range". Hamish Brown, who climbed Scotland's 279 Munros (peaks of 3,000 ft. or more) and wrote a book about it, had a disparaging entry in his log book, "Monadh Liath Puddings". He thought they were the dullest hills in Scotland.

It depends what you are looking for. My trouble is that I *like* plum puddings. The Monadhliaths have been criticised for their "vast and dreary wastes" and their "irksome solitudes", but for those who want to get away from the commercial bedlam of tourist centres like Aviemore the solitude of Strathdearn is its greatest attraction. Brown, the Munro-bagger, may have been influenced by the fact that this is largely Corbett country (Corbetts are hills of 2,500 ft and over) and not Munro country.

Strathdearn forms the upper basin and valley of the River Findhorn. The river was originally called the Earn. Records going back to the twelfth century show the name "Dalfergussyn in Stratherne", and the Gaelic for it is *Fionn-Earn*, the word *fionn* meaning white, which is thought to refer to the Findhorn's turbulent waters. The "white weet" in the Cabrach is nothing compared with the rainfall in the Monadhliaths. It was here, after all, that the Muckle Spate began. Dalfergussyn is Dalarossie, whose old kirk stands where the Findhorn twists into a shepherd's crook a few miles south of Tomatin. Farther on is Coignafearn, one of five Coigs in the glen. The word 'coig' is an old measure of land signifying a fifth. This district was known in the sixteenth and seventeenth centuries as Schepin – the Land of Peace or Fairy Land.

Strathdearn probes into the Monadhliath hills for some fifteen miles and beyond the Coigs the Glen becomes wilder and lonelier. Douglas Simpson called it "the least known and loveliest of Central Highland glens", and he was right. The farther south you go, the more you are drawn into its tranquillity. Over the hills to the east, and at no great distance away, are the crowded ski slopes, the A9, the choked roads, the B&B

Not since the Stuarts had a reigning monarch set foot in Scotland until George IV's arrival at Leith in August, 1822. Here his procession, as portrayed by William Turner, enters Princes Street in Edinburgh. *By courtesy of City of Edinburgh Arts Centre.*

Driving Snow, by Joseph Farquharson, the Laird of Finzean, whose fondness for snow scenes with sheep in them won him the nickname of "Frozen Mutton". *By courtesy of Aberdeen Art Gallery & Museums, Aberdeen City Arts Department.*

Howard Butterworth, the Deeside painter, has a considerable reputation nowadays for his portrayal of glens. Here he paints Glen Muick, where he actually lives, close to Birkhall, home of the Queen Mother, to whom he has sold some of his pictures. *By courtesy of the artist.*

Blair Castle today remains a thriving centre of Highland dancing, piping and fiddle music. A painting by Sir Henry Raeburn of Niel Gow, the legendary fiddler, hangs within. *By courtesy of Perthshire Tourist Board.*

The 4th Duke of Atholl commissioned this painting from Sir Edwin Landseer. Known as *Death of a Hart in Glen Tilt*, it shows the Duke attended by his Head Forester, John Crerar, and keepers. *From His Grace the Duke of Atholl's Collection at Blair Castle, Perthshire.*

Glen Tilt. In Victorian times shooting lodges proliferated in many
Highland glens. It was at Bynack Lodge, at the Deeside end of Glen Tilt, that
Queen Victoria took her leave of the Duke of Atholl when returning from
Blair Castle to Balmoral. *By courtesy of Perthshire Tourist Board.*

When Queen Victoria first came to Balmoral in 1848, she fell in love with
Glen Muick — "so wild and grand". Loch Muick lies in the shadow of Byron's
"Dark Lochnagar". *By courtesy of Scotland in Focus Picture Library.*

From a Victorian artist back to another contemporary one—this time Willie Forbes, formerly Head Stalker on the Mar Lodge Estate, who lives a few miles west of Braemar. Here is a characteristic painting of birds in flight on the heather. *By courtesy of the artist.*

Ancient Dunkeld Cathedral, in its sylvan setting by the Tay. Niel Gow was born at nearby Inver, and Beatrix Potter had her holiday home in the area for many years. *By courtesy of Perthshire Tourist Board.*

guest-houses and the souvenir shops, but they seem a long way off.

The Monadh Liath range runs north-east along the Spey Valley for some thirty miles, stretching from above Garva Bridge, where the Corrieyarick Pass disgorges its travellers into Badenoch, to above Grantown. Queen Victoria travelled along the rim of the Monadhliaths in 1861 and 1873, going through "the very poor long village of Newton More" and seeing "hills rising grandly in the distance", but they were probably the Cairngorms, and it is unlikely that she even knew about the Monadhliaths. There was no mention of them in her *Journal*.

There are plenty of escape routes into the Monadhliaths from Newtonmore and Kingussie. Old tracks and stalkers' paths reach well into the hills; one goes up from Newtonmore by Glen Banchory to Carn Dearg (one of Hamish Brown's Munros), where the Findhorn has its source. If you follow the Abhainn Cro Clach, one of the main headwaters of the river, you eventually reach a path going through Coignafearn Forest, but most tracks tail off before that. For the remaining untracked miles you need heavy boots, a map, a compass, and a strong will.

James Robertson had them all. A botanist, who made this part of the Highlands his stomping ground in the eighteenth century, he set off from Kingussie in 1771 to carry out research in Strathdearn. Although it was June, snow still lay on the hills and he was battered and soaked by an unexpected hailstorm. He tramped for ten miles before, exhausted, he reached the first inhabited place. The cottagers revived him with goat's milk and bread.

Robertson discovered that a wedding was taking place the following day and that the Dalarossie folk were gathering in a nearby cottage for a foot-washing ceremony. He was invited to join them. The celebration went on all night, helped by ample supplies of whisky, and at six o'clock in the morning they sat down to breakfast, which consisted of the insides of a sheep, swimming in fat, followed by curds and cream, then cheese, all washed down with more whisky. After the wedding, the festivities got under way again, breaking for supper – boiled mutton and broth, oatmeal, and more whisky – and finishing at two o'clock the next morning. That day, the 28th, Robertson set off on his travels again, probably more exhausted than he was when he arrived at Dalarossie.

Pitmain, between Kingussie and Newtonmore, was the starting point for Robertson's trek through the Monadhliath hills. Today, it is no more than a name at the end of a farm road, but at one time hundreds of people came from all over the Highlands to the Pitmain Tryst, the annual cattle market held there every September. Elizabeth Grant wrote about it in her *Memoirs of a Highland Lady* in 1814, recalling the dinner after the market, when drovers, farmers and lairds came together "to enjoy the best good cheer the county afforded". There were grand speeches, plenty of punch, and Lord Huntly sent a stag over from the Gaick. There was also an inn at Pitmain. The Pitmain Ball, which followed the Tryst, was held "in the large room at Pitmain", but this may have been one of the farm buildings, for the inn would have been too small for such an event.

It is more than likely that James Robertson stayed at the Pitmain Inn before

Transporting a spinning wheel and its operator across the street outside the Highland Folk Museum at Kingussie. By courtesy of Aberdeen Journals Ltd.

setting off for Strathdearn, for neither Newtonmore nor Kingussie existed at that time. When Elizabeth Grant arrived in 1812, Kingussie was in embryo – "a few very untidy-looking slated stone houses" – and she also saw "a good many black turf huts, frightful without, though warm and comfortable within". Today a replica of one of these "black houses" can be seen at the Highland Folk Museum at Kingussie. Elizabeth spent a night at the Pitmain Inn in 1812 and thought it "wretched" – "no carpets on the floors, no cushions on the chairs, no curtains to the windows".

Colonel Thomas Thornton, the irrepressible English sportsman who went romping around the Highlands in search of game in 1784, mentioned the Pitmain proprietor, "my old landlord, McLean", in his book, *Sporting Tour through the Northern Parts of England and Great Part of the Highlands of Scotland*. He was invited to a ceilidh which, he says, was held, not in the inn, but in a room 50 ft long, normally used as a malt-kiln. Here, the bagpipes skirled, the ladies sang "delightful Erse songs", and the merrymakers toasted "George the Third, long may he reign", with "unfeigned loyalty".

If Elizabeth Grant thought little of the inn at Pitmain, Lord Cockburn, the great Circuit judge, who had a keen eye and a caustic tongue, thought even less. "Old

Pitmain!" he declared. "An abominable hostel." In the days in which the traveller had to pass two nights on the road between Edinburgh and Inverness, even when going by the fastest public coach, Pitmain was the "second house of refuge". "What a scene!" growled his Lordship, describing how coach passengers scrambled from the coach to the inn. "Every monster rushed in and seized whatever he could lay his claws upon – meat, drink, the seat next the fire, the best room, the best bed – and awkwardness or timidity were left to shiver or starve!"

But where exactly was the Pitmain Inn? There seems to be nothing left of the original site, although some people say that the barn at the farm was the scene of Colonel Thornton's grand ceilidh. I found the real answer, or think I did, when I drove past the barn and up to a house at the top of a steep brae. Here I met John Munro, who was factor of a number of Speyside estates, including Pitmain, until he retired in 1975. The Pitmain estate, which covers 12,000 acres, is good grouse territory. It is bounded on the north by Strathdearn, and when John came to Speyside in 1969 there was no one still alive who could remember hearing anything about the old inn. No tales of the Pitmain Tryst had been handed down through the years.

But John has his own theory. He took me down the brae to where the hill outside his garden overlooked the road to Kingussie. There was a kind of rough, overgrown plateau beside the path, with a curious lump in the centre. This, he believes, is where the Pitmain Inn stood, above the barn where they drank King Geordie's health. He pushed his way through some heavy undergrowth to the far side of the knoll, where, hidden in the grass and weeds, there were traces of a track running down to the main road and the entrance to the farm. There was one more piece of the jigsaw to be dropped into place. John told me that the building he lived in at the top of the brae was called the Farmhouse. After his visit to Badenoch in 1844, Lord Cockburn wrote in his diary: "My old friend the inn of Pitmain I found converted into a farm-house."

We stood on the brae and looked out across the Spey towards Glen Feshie. The ghosts of Elizabeth Grant and the irascible Lord Cockburn were peering over our shoulders. Was it really here that they sat, in the old Pitmain Inn, eating grouse from the Pitmain moors, drinking wine and gazing out over the long sweep of the valley to the Cairngorms? There were no polished tables, or even clean ones, at the inn, said Elizabeth, but the dinner on the whole was excellent; hotch-potch, salmon, fine mutton, grouse, scanty vegetables, bad bread, but good wine.

As for Lord Cockburn, even he had a soft spot for the inn, despite his criticism. It had served the public at least one hundred years, he said, and all that time "had received that sort of welcome which is given by a vessel in distress to the only port it has to repair to". With Pitmain closed, he had to go up the road to the Gordon Arms Hotel at Kingussie. It had, he remarked, "the loudest bells and the strongest teethed rats I have ever encountered".

The light was going. Grey wisps of mist had fallen over the hills, and there was a soft, gentle look to the rugged landscape. The whole world seemed still. I said to John Munro that he was lucky to have such a view from his doorstep, but he probably took it for granted. "No," he said. "I never do that." So I said goodbye to him and went off down the brae, heading for Dalwhinnie, following the trail of the drovers who had pushed their black cattle over the Pass of Drumochter to markets in the south. Pitmain was a central point at which cattle could be sold and collected into droves for the long journey to the Falkirk Tryst.

I was in Wade's footsteps again. Down Glen Truim, stretches of the military road came creeping in from the east, from Milehouse of Nuide and Phones, linking up with the Drumochter road at Ettridge. On the outskirts of Dalwhinnie, the A889 turns north to Catlodge, covering the route of the military road, which ran by Sherrabeg and Garva Bridge to the Corrieyairack Pass. The way west today is by the road to Spean Bridge, passing Kinloch Laggan, where a private road runs up the side of Loch Laggan to Ardverikie.

"There is little to say of our stay at Ardverikie," wrote Queen Victoria. "The

Happiness is a chat with the Queen Mum at Crathie, 1987. Courtesy of Aberdeen Journals Ltd.

country is very fine, but the weather was most dreadful." It was the weather that did it, falling in great torrents over Creag Meagaidh, splashing down on Loch Laggan, beating against the old shooting-lodge where Landseer's drawings decorated the walls. In the end, Victoria plumped for Balmoral, and Ardverikie slipped back into its isolation.

Yet today, when thousands of people turn up at Crathie on Deeside every Sunday to watch the Queen going to kirk, and when newspapers keep a relentless eye on their activities, some members of the Royal Family must wish that their Victorian ancestors had made a different choice. Prince Albert wrote of Ardverikie: "The reporters call it an 'un-come-at-able' place, because they are quartered on the other side of Loch Laggan, which is only to be crossed on a flying bridge that belongs exclusively to ourselves." The flying bridge was a floating bridge, later replaced by an iron bridge.

Prince Albert's "un-come-at-able" quote was from the *Illustrated London News*, whose correspondent was clearly disenchanted with Ardverikie. It was so difficult to find, he said, that anyone seeking "the enchanted castle of Ardverikie" would probably be found years later "a mouldering skeleton, grasping an 'Anderson's guide to the Highlands' in one hand and an empty whisky flask in the other, having set out years before to have a look at the Hunting Quarters of the Queen".

Even a century and a half ago, Royalty's relations with the Press were strained. The Prince Consort's attitude to the Press has its counterpart in the Duke of Edinburgh's ill-concealed dislike for inquisitive reporters. Albert was delighted by Ardverikie's seclusion; he was probably remembering Blair Castle a few years earlier, when every move was watched by reporters. It was said that *The Times* reporter was up at five o'clock in the morning, peeping through the park palings, while the *Morning Post* reporter hid himself in a bed of nettles to see the Queen emerge. At Ardverikie, denied any copy worth publishing, the newspapermen were irritated by Prince Albert's smugness. "The Prince looked pleased with everything, and everybody, and himself too," wrote one reporter.

One wonders what today's scandal-chasing tabloids would have made of young Claud Hamilton, who disgraced himself in front of Queen Victoria at Ardverikie. Four-year-old Claud was a son of Lord Abercorn, who had rented the deer forest there and built the shooting-lodge. When the Queen stayed at Loch Laggan he was moved from his nursery to cramped quarters in the home farm. He resented his eviction and when he was presented to the Queen he refused to bow – instead, he stood on his head. The result was that her Majesty discovered what a young Highlander wore – or didn't wear – under his kilt. She was not amused. Later, taken back to the Queen to apologise, he did it again.

Baring his bottom to the Sovereign didn't mar Claud's future prospects. When he grew up he became Lord Claud Hamilton, a Member of Parliament, a Lord of the Treasury – and an ADC to the Queen. His brother, Lord Frederick Hamilton, said in his memoirs, "I believe that he would still do it today, more than seventy-five years later".

When Queen Victoria went over the Pass of Drumochter to Blair in 1861 she spent a night at the Loch Ericht Hotel at Dalwhinnie. It was formerly a Government

The present-day Drumochter Pass on the A9 route. Well-surfaced, but treacherous and sometimes closed in winter.

inn and the Queen was not impressed by it. "There was hardly anything to eat," she wrote, "and there was only tea, and two miserable starved Highland chickens, without any potatoes! No pudding and no *fun*; no little maid (the two there not wishing to come in), nor our two people – who were wet and drying out their things – to wait on us! It was not a nice supper."

Today, a modern extension has been built on to the original hotel. The marriage of old and new has produced a curious architectural hybrid. There would probably be some highly critical comment from Prince Charles if he ever stayed there, but at least he would not be fed on two starved Highland chickens. If the hotel is an unattractive building, Dalwhinnie itself is even less attractive, a straggling, raggle-taggle town which sits in a kind of dazed uncertainty between the railway and the motorway, belonging to neither.

Yet it has always been a cross-roads for traffic passing through the Highlands, the apex of a rough triangle formed by both old and new roads. It has seen a passing parade of drovers, roadbuilders, whisky smugglers, commercial travellers and "a variety of vagrants such as gypsies, ragmen, vendors of crockery, tinsmiths, egg dealers and old clothes men". Joseph Mitchell, whose father, John Mitchell, worked for Thomas Telford and became one of the leading roadbuilders of his time, wrote of commercial travellers who still rode on horseback after the roads were complete – "portly old gentlemen with

Deserted cottages fast falling into ruin near the Drumochter Summit.

rubicund faces who wore top hats, blue coats with brass buttons; rode good horses, did their business in no hurry, had saddlebags behind for their cloths and samples and carried large whips."

Over the years, on good roads and bad, the English came north to explore darkest Scotland: men like William Larkin, author of *A Tour in the Highlands of Scotland*, who in 1818, noting the growing tourist traffic, said that "a fund of good temper" was required on routes where inns were liable to be crowded at certain seasons of the year. At Dalwhinnie, tempers became frayed when the grouse-shooting season coincided with the arrival of drovers on their way to the Falkirk Tryst.

In 1840, the ubiquitous Lord Cockburn, off on another of his Circuits, wrote about the extraordinary number of foreign travellers, mostly English, who "fill every conveyance, and every inn, attracted by scenery, curiosity, and superfluous time and wealth, while, attracted by grouse, the mansion houses of half our poor devils of Highland lairds are occupied by rich and titled Southrons". If his ghost *still* looks over our shoulders, his Lordship will be surprised to learn that not much has changed in the last century and a half.

The roads brought new life to the Highlands, but it was the coming of the railways that brought the biggest change. On September 9, 1863, the Highland Railway was officially opened – and the first "iron horse" steamed up Drumochter. Lord Cockburn thought that the country had become "an asylum of railway lunatics", but one result of the railway mania was that the remote Scottish glens had become more accessible to Cockburn's "Southrons". The rush to the moors had begun – the hunters were coming.

CHAPTER 6

ROYAL HUNTERS

FROM THE OUTSKIRTS OF BLAIR, dodging the rush of traffic, I crossed the busy A9, scrambled over a fence, and began to climb the Hill of Tulloch. It was the same route that Queen Victoria had taken when she made her way up the hill in 1842, but there was no traffic then. She had to go through a cabbage-field, and she was on the back of a pony led by a servant in Highland dress. His name was Sandy McAra, and when they forded the River Garry at the bottom of the hill the water came up over his knees. Today you can cross by a bridge. The Queen saw sheep grazing on the hill – "pretty Highland sheep" – and her bird's-eye view of Blair made the houses "look like little toys". It was, she said, the most romantic ride and walk she had ever had.

Looking down on that scene a century and a half later, it seemed that not much had changed; not, at any rate, from a distance. From where the Queen stood she could see the Falls of Bruar, and Dalnacardoch, where Wade had begun his great road to Crieff, and old Beinn a' Ghlo, the mountain of the mist, standing guard on Thomas Pennant's "horrible" Glen Tilt. The Tilt is a turbulent stream. It was deep and almost impassable when Victoria forded it at the dangerous Poll Tarff in 1862 – "nearly up to the men's waists", she wrote in her *Journal*. Sandy McAra was again the guide, getting his feet wet a second time.

Beinn a' Ghlo, 3,671 ft high, lords it over the Forest of Atholl which was once described as a "treeless barren waste of mountain country". It stretches from Glenshee in the east to the Garry in the west, and northwards from Blair to the Inverness and Aberdeenshire boundaries. Today the estate covers 135,000 acres, including the deer forests. There are nineteen corries in Beinn a' Ghlo, and they say that a rifle can be fired in any one of them without being heard in another.

The Forest of Atholl has always been an important hunting ground. It was here that some of the great Tinchels of the sixteenth century took place. In this form of hunting, five or six hundred men spread themselves over an area seven or eight miles wide and chased the deer to a point where the hunters were waiting. Queen Mary watched a Tinchel in Atholl in 1563, and one of the most magnificent hunts ever held there was organised in 1528 in honour of James V, who was visiting Atholl with his mother.

Stag shot by Prince Albert, 4 October, on Corrie-na-Poitch, and Donald Stewart, one of the foresters. Balmoral, 5 October 1854. Photograph by George Washington Wilson. Reproduced by courtesy of the Royal Archives, Windsor Castle.

The Earl of Atholl set out to please his Royal guests, feeding them "all manner of meates and delicates" – venison, goose, capon, swan, partridge, plover, duck, muirfowl (grouse), peacocks; the list goes on and on. This kind of self-indulgence wasn't unusual. John Taylor, the Water Poet, joined a hunting party on the Braes of Mar in 1618 and recorded with lip-licking relish the food they ate – venison, roast beef, mutton, goats, kid, hares, fresh salmon, pigeons, chickens, partridge, capercaillies and heathcocks. Nor was there a shortage of drink. King James could choose from ale, beer, wine, hippocras, malmesy and muskadel, while the Water Poet helped himself to "good ales, sack, white and claret, tent (or Alicante), with most potent *Aquavitae*".

I once sat on the cliffs above Loch Einich in the Cairngorms thinking of Colonel Thomas Thornton, who, after shooting ptarmigan on the Einich plateau, consumed a hearty dinner not far from where I was eating my corned beef sandwich. His chief dish, he recorded, consisted of "two brace and a half of ptarmigans and a moorcock, a quarter of a pound of butter, some slices of Yorkshire smoked ham, and a reindeer's tongue, with some sweet herbs, pepper, etc". He finished his meal with "snow-cooled champagne and sherbet". I finished mine with a cup of tea and followed the Colonel's spectral footsteps down to the loch.

While Victorian appetites never reached the gluttonous proportions of those earlier days, the sportsmen of last century were no less anxious to have a few home comforts when out shooting. The result was that shooting lodges, or boxes, as the smaller lodges were called, sprouted in many remote glens. The ruins of some of them can still be seen today, their well-cut granite blocks hinting at an unexpected solidity and comfort. Geldie Lodge, with its shattered walls and faint air of lost elegance, lies off the road to Glen Feshie; it was said to be the most westerly house in Aberdeenshire. The ruins of Bynack Lodge, where Queen Victoria took her leave of the Duke of Atholl when returning from Blair Castle, can be found just south of the Geldie, at the Deeside end of Glen Tilt. At Bachnagairn, high on the cleft of the South Esk, fragments of a wall and a fireplace are all that is left of a lodge built by Sir Alan Russell Mackenzie, 2nd Baronet, in Glenmuick. It is a lonely spot, but a lovely one, inspiring one poet to write about the yellow, winding pathway that leads to "the Paradise o' Pines at Bachnagairn". Across the hills, deep in the heart of Glen Ey, is Altanour Lodge, crumbling away in an eerie setting of dead trees. There are many more.

Here, in these old, forgotten lodges, the gentry ate, drank and relaxed after a day on the moors. In Glen Bruar, classic ground to the deerstalker, there are the remains of the original Bruar Lodge, which William Scrope wrote about in his *Days of Deerstalking*. No monarch, he said, ever entered a palace or any lady a ballroom with more delight than that which he felt when he entered his "lonely abode" at Bruar. Even when the wind blew under the door and stirred the carpet into chilly life, the tablecloth never budged – "the weight of the meal made it retain its station", said Scrope. Few, if any, of the lodges had bathrooms, although there were plenty of hip baths, and King Edward VII often took his own bath with him when he went to stay with friends. Perhaps he inherited this fastidiousness from Prince Albert, who always went shooting as if dressed for a stroll in the garden. In those days, a frock coat and patent leather shoes were the order of the day for the well-dressed sportsman.

So, wined, dined and literally dressed to kill, off they went in search of prey. Royalty had its own lodges – Glas-allt Shiel and Allt-na-guibhsaich are two that are seen by visitors to Loch Muick on the Balmoral estate. From these and other shiels the Royal hunters went out to the moors with their guns ready. It was in Strathgirnock on 30 September, 1860, that the Prince of Wales, later King Edward VII, made a record for a single day's stalking in the Balmoral deer forest by grassing eight stags in the corrie of the Boultsach.

Mar Lodge, near Braemar, whose foundation stone was laid by Queen Victoria in 1895, also saw some crack shooting. It was on this estate that the Duke of Fife brought down twenty-two stags in one day, forty-five over three days. The Duke held the record

Deer on the track to Loch Muick. In winter they come down to feed at the Spittal of Glen Muick. The narrow path climbing up from the far end of the loch is one of two routes to the Broad Cairn, where a track goes by Bachnagairn to Glen Cova.

for the number of stags killed in one man's lifetime. The figure is given as "about 4,000" – presumably the Duke lost count in the end. Mar Lodge and Invercauld are still two of the biggest shooting estates on Deeside. The Mar estate was bought in 1961 by two Swiss brothers, Gerald and John Paunchaud, both now dead. A few months before Gerald Paunchaud's death in 1989 the estate was bought by an American billionaire, John Kluge.

The Duke of Leeds, who at one time leased Mar Lodge, held a deer drive – an old-fashioned Tinchell – in Glen Quoich in 1850, with Queen Victoria, the Prince Consort and the Prince of Wales as his guests. A herd of 300 deer passed within a short distance of the Royal party and it was estimated that there were no fewer than 3,000 deer in the glen. The wind changed and the herd broke up, 800 going off by another pass. Tables and chairs were brought by ponies for the picnic that followed, but Victoria had *her* food sitting in the heather.

Mar Lodge saw an even older form of hunting in 1822. That year, the Earl of Fife reintroduced wild boars into the forest, and in October a wild boar hunt was held, using staghounds and greyhounds for the chase. Both the animal's tusks were shot off by one of the guests, Lord Kennedy, and when the boar was eventually brought down it had to

dismal silence while a London season has been flirting and fluttering the days away."

Lord Granville attempted to describe the excitement of a grouse shoot at the beginning of this century – "See! the birds are coming straight for you: a hundred thousand forms seem to float in the air with motionless wings. You pick out one which seems first; no, there are others before him. You change your mind and your bird. Bang! … missed him. Bang! … missed again. Bang! Bang! … not a feather is ruffled, and the whole pack skims away to the glen behind". But not every shot was a miss. The toll of grouse in the early days was high – 10,600 birds were killed at Glenbucket in 1872, and a "bag" of 7,000 birds was chalked up over the season at Delnadamph, where Prince Charles frequently goes shooting today.

Granville Gordon, banging away at his "hundred thousand forms" floating in the air, thought that Scotland was "one vast game farm, a pleasure retreat for sportsmen with their friends and families". In these days of national nature reserves and comparatively free access to the hills, his views seem hugely outdated. He regarded any attempt to open up the hills to the public as "handing over to the mob". He obviously thought that the masses should be grateful that the lairds and their ladies used the countryside as a "pleasure retreat". If private ownership was abolished and the estates

The hunters and the ghillie … a striking picture of Victorian sportsmen relaxing during a fishing expedition.

The bag after a day on the Donside moors … a picture that captures the atmosphere of the old-time grouse shoots. The picture was shown at the Corgarff Rural Exhibition.

nationalised, Aberdonians would descend on the Dee Valley "with Mauser rifles, guns and salmon rods". Aboyne would be badly hit – "the hotel keeper, the tailor, bootmaker, the chemist who sells cold cream, golf balls, aerated waters and tobacco".

The threat of nationalisation was often in the minds of the lairds. In Blair Cast. there is a picture of Lloyd George riding across the Atholl moors on the back of a pony like some latter-day Sancho Panza, coat flapping, hat pulled down, legs stuck out like ramrods. Walking with him is John, 8th Duke of Atholl, whose wife, Katherine, was the famous "Red Duchess", M.P. for Kinross and West Perthshire from 1923-38. Lloyd George had been toying with the idea of turning deer forests into smallholdings and the Duke invited him to Blair to see the moors for himself. Maybe it was the pony ride that did it, for the little Welshman dropped the plan.

Even today, however, there are lairds who still regard their estates as "pleasure

Derry Lodge, now ruinous, stands at the meeting point of the Derry Burn and the Linn Water in the Forest of Mar. This nineteenth-century stone building was once a favourite shooting lodge of Queen Victoria. Courtesy of Aberdeen Journals Ltd.

retreats", out of bounds to climbers and hillwalkers. The old conflict over rights of way rumbles on. Only a few years ago, Gerald Paunchaud at Mar Lodge was looked upon as the hillwalkers' mortal enemy, totally opposed to anything that might disturb his deer. He was held responsible for the deterioration of Derry Lodge, which was at one time leased to the Cairngorm Club. The Lodge in its heyday is seen in a picture in which a kilted Prince of Wales (later Edward VII) is standing at the door of the building with a house party. Now it is virtually a ruin.

Our old friend Lord Cockburn was on the side of the untitled masses. In 1846, he complained that travellers in search of such innocent things as botany, geology or scenery were "stopped by his Grace the Duke of Leeds, the tacksman of the Mar Lodge shootings, who says he has a right to protect the deer from disturbance". The public, added Lord Cockburn, said he had no such right. "Then, at this lower end of the glen another Grand Duke – he of Atholl – has been pleased to set his gates and his keepers, and for the same reason, that he may get more deer to shoot easily."

The Duke of Atholl got his come-uppance in 1847, when a famous legal action was brought by the Scottish Rights of Way Society after Professor J. Hutton Balfour, Professor of Botany at Edinburgh University, was halted by the Duke's keepers while on his way through Glen Tilt with a party of students. The Professor stood his ground, his attitude being summed up in Sir Douglas Maclagan's "Ballad of Glen Tilt":

> For Dukes shall we
> Care a'e bawbee?
> The road's as free
> To you and me
> As to his Grace himself, man.

It was a sentiment shared by the court, who found in favour of the Scottish Rights of Way Society. One wonders what his Grace would have said if he could have peeped into his crystal ball and seen Blair Castle 143 years later, with walkers tramping freely through Glen Tilt and the 10th Duke of Atholl opening up his 700-year-old home to thousands of visitors every year.

Four years before the Glen Tilt case, Lord Cockburn had some harsh words to say about the Duke's father, Lord Glenlyon, who had run the estate when his brother was confined to a lunatic asylum. Glenlyon apparently warned off strangers by having threatening placards "at every corner". Lord Cockburn remarked that "very few of the owners of our great places have sense or humanity to make the enjoyment of their places by others a source of enjoyment to themselves". It may be that the Glen Tilt case was a watershed, for few lairds are likely to go to such lengths today, whatever their views on hill-walkers and botanists.

Not all the Atholl lairds were as intransigent as either Lord Glenlyon or the Duke who played villain in the "Ballad of Glen Tilt". Lord Cockburn pointed out that the grandfather of the "ballad Duke" had a totally different attitude, and, in fact, made a drive several miles up the glen, although he was "by far the greatest deer-killer in

Scotland". He not only permitted, but encouraged, strangers to use it freely. Lord Cockburn, who had never seen Glen Tilt, applied for a pass to go up the glen in his carriage. "I wrote a note with respectful compliments," he said, "re-duking and re-gracing him, and humbly begging that such a worm might be permitted to set his base wheels on this once free drive." He got his pass.

When I was up on the Hill of Tulloch, I traced out the path taken by Queen Victoria on her way back to Blair Castle after her pony-trekking climb. In the distance, across the River Garry, was the ancient lairdship of Lude, which I first came to know some years ago when I was following the trail of the Marquis of Montrose in his Covenanting wars. It was a mile north of Lude House that James Graham met his raggle-taggle army of Highlanders and raised the Royal Standard in 1644.

But I was thinking of another kind of "battle" when I saw Lude. If the Atholl lairds had trouble with intruders on their land, they had even more problems with their neighbours at Lude. Lord Cockburn commented on the fact that Blair had two hotels within 300 yards of each other: one of the effects, he said, of a "ridiculous rivalship" between the houses of Atholl and Lude. "Each laird built his inn, and his village," said Cockburn", "and Lude consoled itself for Athole's getting the church by Lude getting the poor bit of an Episcopal chapel."

The Blair–Lude dispute was certainly the longest, although it affected different lairds. It began as far back as the late seventeenth century, when Atholl foresters reported driving livestock belonging to Robertson of Lude out of the Forest of Atholl. It died down and flared up again in the eighteenth century – "There's a fresh war broke out in the Forest of Atholl", said one report – and the start of the nineteenth century still saw the two sides at each others' throats.

The only arms ever used were seven or eight cannons ornamenting the lawn at Lude House. For reasons that are unclear, the Duke of Atholl was awarded a court decree giving him the right to shoot over Lude. He immediately set out to annoy his neighbour, General Robertson of Lude, by holding a day's deer-shooting over his land. The General, however, had the last word – or last shot. He loaded the cannons on his lawn and proceeded to fire them at regular intervals throughout the day. The result was that the deer disappeared and the Atholl hunters were left empty-handed.

The Battle of Blair entered a new phase in 1821, when James McInroy of Lude bought the estate. Relationships worsened rather than improved, and when McInroy died and his son took over they became even more fragile. In 1889, the Duke of Atholl and William McInroy of Lude went to court over the Crom Altan Pass on Beinn a' Ghlo. McInroy claimed that the pass was a public right of way and when the nineteenth century died the dispute was still grumbling on.

The lairds were also plagued by poachers and smugglers. It was not simply a case of rabbit for the pot, or even an occasional deer. One Braemar poacher had a bag of 300 stags and hinds in ten years – an average of thirty a year. The law on poaching was so vague that foresters (gamekeepers) were instructed merely to ask the suspect's name and, if he refused to give it, follow him and do their best to identify him. In 1770, when a forester challenged four army officers found shooting on the Atholl moors, they asked if he had a warrant from the Duke to stop them. He said that he *did* have a warrant – and they told him to stick it up his backside.

John Crerar, head forester at Atholl, wrote to the Duke on 24 February, 1882:

> I had a line from McIntire, who says the House of Filar has been Broak, and Eighteen Bottles of Wine drunk; porter, hams and other things eat or taken. He thinks the smuglars were the rogs, as sume of them comming through Pool Tarff the other week lost a horse getting through the foard, the water was so high.

The "Filar" of Crerar's letter is Fealar, a remote lodge in Atholl's Faith Lair, about twenty miles from Pitlochry. The dissolute Lord Kennedy rented Fealar from the Duke of Atholl. It was while there in 1822 that he wagered 2,000 guineas that between midnight on 12 August, the Glorious Twelfth, and midnight the following day he could kill forty brace of grouse, ride to his seat at Dunnottar, and ride back to Fealar. He started shooting at four o'clock in the morning and shot the whole forty brace in 4 hr 41 min. He covered 154 miles on horseback and completed his task in fifteen hours and fifty-six minutes.

Lord Kennedy had a gamekeeper called Alexander Davidson, a crack shot, who became one of the North-east's legendary poachers, his territory covering a massive area of Forfarshire, Aberdeenshire and Banffshire, as well as cutting into Inverness-shire and the north of Perthshire. He was drawn into one of Lord Kennedy's bets when he agreed to run naked from Barclay Street in Stonehaven to Inchmarlo on Deeside, a distance of about 25 miles. Lord Kennedy, along with Farquharson of Finzean, had actually wagered that Davidson would never make it, and had hired a group of women, armed with stones, to waylay him at the bridge at Banchory. When Davidson saw them he put his head down and charged them like a mad bull. He made it across the bridge and reached Inchmarlo well within the time.

Sandy Davidson, who was found dead in the hills of Glenbuchat with his faithful brown pointer at his side, took part in whisky smuggling before turning to poaching, and he may well have known about an incident mentioned in another letter from John Crerar to the Duke of Atholl in the year of the Kennedy wager:

> Beginning of last week there came three Boats full with Whisky; sum where below the joining of the Tumble and the Gary. At the Boat of Port na Craige one of the boats Left upon a rock, overstett, one man lost, one got out by one of the oars, the third By a hold of one of the Barrels of Whisky. I hear since the other two Boats were taken about Stanley with their Cargos by the Excise.

The Royal hunters, the whisky smugglers, the foresters, the poachers ... they all have their place in the corridors of Blair Castle, where paintings, photographs and a fascinating

array of exhibits are on show. Here, up to 150 people work each summer to give visitors a taste of Atholl history. The Atholl Highlanders lined up in Dunkeld and marched through the town with Queen Victoria when she arrived there in 1842; now a modern generation of Highlanders parades twice a year for the benefit of tourists from all over the world. As many as 2,000 visitors have attended the Athollmen's parade in May.

But it is out in the hills that the Atholl story comes alive, up the long road to Forest Lodge and the Falls of Tarff and on through the wedge of hills at the Allt Garbh Buidhe to Bynack and the Geldie. Victoria went this way in 1861, heading home from Blair, with the Duke of Atholl at her side. Sandy McAra was still there, now headkeeper, but grown old and grey. The Duke led the way, but at the Poll Tarff the Queen told him that Sandy had better take his place. They plunged into the water with the pipers still playing.

The names come creeping out of the past in these Atholl lands … Carn a' Chlamain, where the Queen, sitting with her sketchbook, marvelled at the sense of solitude; Glen Chroine, called the Sanctum, a haunt of red deer; Fealar, where the whisky smugglers drank eighteen bottles of wine; "Bainoch" (Bynack), where the Queen and Albert drank whisky out of the Duke's old silver flask and the Highlanders shouted a Gaelic greeting before taking their leave of the Royal guests; and a hill which the Queen called "Scarsach", where the boundaries of Perth, Aberdeen and Inverness came together.

Grass and berries grow on the upper slopes of Victoria's "Scarsach" – 3,300 ft An Sgarsoch – and there is a tradition that at one time a cattle and horse fair was held on its summit. There are said to be traces of a stone causeway on the hill. From the top of An Sgarsoch you can look west to the head waters of the River Feshie. It was through Glen Feshie that Queen Victoria went on a trip that took her to Speyside and down by the Pass of Drumochter to Blair Atholl.

An imposing view of Blair Castle during the presentation of a seat by the Scottish Scouts Association to the Duke of Atholl. Courtesy of Aberdeen Journals Ltd.

CHAPTER 7

WILD YOUNG WOMEN

MIST HUNG IN A GREY PALL OVER GLEN FESHIE, wet and depressing. The Queen, wrapped in a plaid and waterproofs, sat on her pony with her umbrella over her head, the rain beating down on it, the wind throwing up great sprays of water from pools on the track. For all the concern she showed she might have been riding in the park at Windsor. It was her third Great Expedition into the hills, and her second into a wilderness that a Gaelic poet described as *Gleann Feisidh nan siantan* – "Glen Feshie of storm-blasts".

The Queen was riding through a glen steeped in history and tradition. It was through Glen Feshie that the drovers came in the old days, pushing their cattle south by the Feshie-Geldie pass to Blair Atholl, or skirting the mouth of the Lairig Ghru on their way to the Linn of Dee. The road through Glen Feshie was also a raiders' route, and it was to combat their activities that General George Wade set up a garrison in Glen Feshie in 1747.

Jogging along on her pony, marking off the miles from the Dee to the Spey, the Queen was riding in the shadow of a dream that first took shape more than two centuries ago and has haunted the minds of planners ever since. General Wade planned to build a road from Ruthven Barracks to Braemar, following the old driving route through Glen Feshie, but nothing ever came of it. Yet the idea never died. Back in the 1950s, when the plan was dusted off for a modern generation of travellers, author Nigel Tranter led a campaign – the Glen Feshie Road Campaign – to have the highway built. It would follow the old route, but now it would link up with the Newtonmore–Spean Bridge road to Fort William.

Thirty years later, Tranter recalled the campaign in his book, *Nigel Tranter's Scotland*: "I took up this fight because of the obvious need," he wrote, "and because of the magnificent and almost unknown empty country it would open up to visitors, for the head of Feshie in especial is tremendous in scale and dramatic qualities; the yawning abyss of Coire Garbhlach, surely one of the most impressive corries in the land; the remote and exciting course of the River Eidart, perhaps the least known major stream in Scotland, and the Feshie itself."

Today the dream is as far away as ever, and that may be a good thing. The drovers have long since gone, Geldie Lodge has vanished, the old bridge over the Geldie Burn has disappeared, and Bynack Lodge, where Queen Victoria took her leave of the Duke of Atholl after riding through Glen Tilt, lies in ruins. There are no new roads; or, at any rate, only the bulldozed roads that scar the hills in the name of sport.

"Even a sheep path is almost a rarity over these wild mountains," wrote Charles Matthews, the architect and actor, in 1833. The tracks that spread east from Drumochter and Atholl to Deeside and Speyside were beaten out of the heather by drovers and itinerant packmen. When the first of the sportsmen arrived in the early 1800s, the country began to open up, but the roads were still bad and maps were often unreliable. The hills were alien and uninviting; all that people knew about their summits were their strange Gaelic names (the Queen invariably got them wrong in her *Journal*), and when the Royal travellers rode to Inchrory they had to ask the people if there was "any way of getting round over the hills".

Nevertheless, the Queen's "great expeditions" were well organised – open four-wheeled carriages called "sociables" took them on the first stage of their journey, ponies were waiting to carry them into the hills, keepers and servants attended to their needs, and overnight stays were arranged at remote inns – but in an age when ladies were more at home in drawing rooms than deer forests they were remarkable outings. The weather was rarely kind; when they climbed Ben Macdhhui the mist was so thick they could scarcely see the people in front of them. More often than not it rained, frequently it was cold. The Queen, said one lady-in-waiting, "quite accepts the idea of sitting for hours perishing on a pony going at a foot's pace and coming home frozen".

Apart from her own "great expeditions", Victoria accompanied Prince Albert on some of his stalking expeditions, frequently sketching the stags he shot. The killing of deer seemed to leave the Queen unmoved, although she was said to "shake and be very uncomfortable" when Albert took pot-shots at stags from the window of Blair Castle. But she herself never fired a shot, preferring to play the role of an observer with a sketchbook. She believed that ladies who went hunting were "wild young women who are really unsexed".

There were, however, plenty of other emancipated women who were anxious to prove that hunting was not a male prerogative. The magazine *Punch* tilted at these "new women" (one cartoon showed a mournful ghillie weighed down with coats and cloaks and a picnic basket), but Herbert Byng Hall, writing in the 1840s, described them as "a charming addition to the delights of a shooting excursion", while Sir John Astley drooled delicately over the thought of how a lady in a "well-turned out walking-costume, with skirt short enough to prevent its dragging in the mud, treats you to a glimpse of the well-turned ankle and arched instep".

A number of women contributed more to the hunting scene than a well-turned ankle. One was Mrs Ross, wife of the celebrated nineteenth-century marksman, Horatio Ross, who rented the Fealar shooting from the Duke of Atholl and also shot over the Mar deer forest. "In 1851 I shot 118 deer in Mar forest," he said in a letter to a friend. "During that season I killed thirteen in one day, with fourteen chances."

The stories about Horatio Ross are legion, but no one seems to have taken a great deal of notice of his wife's achievements. Patricia Lindsay said in her *Recollections of a Royal Parish* in 1902 that Mrs Ross was "rather a celebrity" on Deeside. "Deerstalking was her favourite pastime," she wrote, "and she was a splendid markswoman." Mrs Lindsay, putting male chauvinism in its place, added almost as an afterthought: "Her husband, too, was a crack shot".

It was the social scene that women dominated during the shooting season, among them the "venerable Duchess of Abercorn", a graceful dancer in her youth; Lady Alicia Gordon, who stayed with her brother, Sir Robert Gordon, at Balmoral and was a popular hostess; the Duke and Duchess of Leeds, who lived in Old Mar Lodge for many years and gathered around them a circle of artistic and sporting guests; and the Dowager Duchess of Athole, who lived to be over ninety and was one of Queen Victoria's closest friends. The Dunkeld coach was named "The Duchess of Athole". It started from an inn called "The Duke's Arms", and a notice advertising the service read: "'The Duchess of Athole' leaves 'The Duke's Arms' every lawful morning at six o'clock".

The Duchess of Athole told this story to Queen Victoria, who thought it highly amusing, but it is unlikely that she was amused by the tale of another Duchess who was drawn, or gently pushed, into another Duke's arms. This was the Duchess of Abercorn's mother, Georgiana, Duchess of Bedford. She was one of Queen Victoria's "wild young women", but, contrary to the Queen's theory that ladies who went shooting were undersexed, this "bold, bad woman", as one diarist described her, was highly sexed. She was a keen sportswoman and, according to Patricia Lindsay, "tramped the heather like a man", but she also had a sharp eye for the opposite sex. She stalked men with the same determination that she hunted deer.

Mrs Lindsay called her the "eccentric Duchess of Bedford". She was the daughter of Jane, Duchess of Gordon, who once recruited a regiment of Gordon Highlanders by offering a guinea and a kiss to every recruit. She was still in a kissing mood when George IV came to Scotland, for she puzzled the King by inviting him to "Come prie my mou, my canty callant". It was the old Scots way of offering *him* a kiss – "Come taste my mouth, my canty callant". Her daughter, Georgiana, was just as willing to let eager suitors "prie her mou'". She often reminded partners at a ball that it was customary for a man to salute his lady with a kiss before the start of a reel.

Georgiana's mother was a determined matchmaker. She married off two of her daughters to the Dukes of Richmond and Manchester and succeeded in persuading Georgiana to marry the widowed 6th Duke of Bedford. It was scarcely the perfect marriage for this swan-like enchantress, who found herself wed to a shy, staid man fourteen years her senior. She produced ten children, eight of them by her husband. The other two, Alexander, born in 1821, and Rachel, born in 1826, were fathered by

Edwin Landseer, the painter, who was besotted by her dark beauty. Their affair, which began when Georgiana was already the mother of eight children, lasted in a spasmodic way until her death.

For a time, news of the liaison simmered quietly under the surface, but in 1823 it came into the open when a scandalsheet called *The Satirist* carried a piece which read: "The Duchess of Bedford has suddenly taken ill in Ireland. Strong draughts were resorted to which relieved the patient. Edwin Landseer is her Grace's draughtsman."

The Duchess had to cope with this type of gossip, as well as suggestions that she was "vulgar-minded", a "wicked woman", and "coquette la lune". Despite it all, the Duke of Bedford adored her and gave her anything she wanted, including a summer retreat at the Doune in Rothiemurchus. Before this, Lady Georgiana and her mother, who had separated from the Duke of Gordon, spent their summers at an old farmhouse at Kinrara, a "but and ben" across the Spey from the Doune. They converted a barn into a "barracks" for the ladies and a stable for the men, made one of the outbuildings a kitchen where the Duchess's French cook prepared *entrées* in an old black potato pot, and turned the old kitchen into a sitting-room. Long James, a servant described by Elizabeth Grant of Rothiemurchus as a "very handsome, impudent person", played the fiddle for guests who wanted to dance.

"Half the London world of fashion, all the clever people that could be hunted out from all parts, all the north country, all the neighbourhood from far and near without regard to wealth or station, flocked to this encampment in the wilderness." wrote Elizabeth Grant in her *Memoirs of a Highland Lady*. They came to enjoy "the free life, the pure air, and the wit and fun the Duchess brought with her to the mountains".

It was at the Doune that Georgiana gave herself over to another kind of emotional commitment, one, perhaps, that was more deeply rooted than her up-and-down relationship with "Lanny". She became more and more attached to the wild and beautiful country that had become her second home – "a passion for the heather", was how Sir Walter Scott described her feelings for it. It opened up new horizons, gave her fresh perspectives, and let her live a life uncluttered by social conventions, which was what she wanted. The "encampment" at Kinrara was her blueprint for the future. Long before Queen Victoria set out on her Great Expeditions, the "bold, bad" Duchess of Bedford was heading in to the Cairngorm hills to pitch her tents, build her bothies, and enjoy the "free life" that she had first tasted at Kinrara. She found her idyll in Glen Feshie, the Glen of the Fairy Stream.

The approach to Glen Feshie by the Geldie is uninspiring, a boggy canvas of dreary moorland reaching up to two outliers of Beinn Bhrotain called Cairn Geldie (2,039 ft) and the Duke's Chair (2,010 ft). The "chair" was called after the Duke of Leeds, presumably because he shot in this area when he had the lease of Mar Forest. The ruins of Geldie Lodge lie on the south bank of the Geldie Burn, which turns away from the Feshie track a short distance beyond the lodge.

From there to the River Eidart the route lies through a monotony of heather, the hills to the north climbing away to 3,651 ft Monadh Mor and to Moine Mhor, a vast expanse of turf and moss which is a favourite haunt of deer. Looking out over Moine Mhor, the Great Moss, you cannot fail to be awed by the immensity of the Cairngorms. From Moine Mhor a track runs down to the Feshie, where a bridge crosses the river to Glenfeshie Lodge.

Down in the glen, the Feshie and Eidart come tumbling down to meet each other. It is almost as if the fairy of *Gleann Feisidh* had waved her magic wand and transformed the scene. High hills close in on either side of the river, then the landscape changes, entering the flats and wandering languorously through a setting of ancient pines and junipers. Back in the 1920s, A. I. McConnochie said in his *Deer and Deer Forests of Scotland* that a thousand deer could be seen on these flats at the beginning of the season. He called it "an oasis in the desert". Its name is Ruigh-aiteachain.

Here, among the junipers and pine trees, the Duchess of Bedford built her encampment, a village of rough huts made of turf, with roofs of unpeeled birch. One building had three or four bedrooms and a kitchen, while two smaller buildings each had one room. The bedrooms had room enough to turn around in, no more. Inside, peat

"The Oasis in the Desert". A sketch of the Duchess of Bedford's encampment as it appeared in the 1830s, when it was said to resemble "a small Indian settlement". Later Queen Victoria wrote in her *Journal*: "The huts, surrounded by magnificent fir trees … looked lovelier than ever. We gazed with sorrow at their utter ruin".

fires blazed away on the ground. Charles Mathews, the architect, who stayed there in 1833, said it was like "a small Indian settlement". The rest of the settlement was made up of tents – the men's quarters. Each tent contained two small leather couches, side by side on trestles, a small table, a washhand basin on a stand, and a foot bath. A number of wardrobes stood on carpets made of turf.

The encampment must have been enlarged after Mathews' visit, for half a dozen huts can be seen in a sketch by Landseer, who spent a great deal of his time in Glen Feshie. He stayed for a period in Glenfeshie Lodge and painted on the west side of the river, but after the Duchess had leased the forest and built her encampment at Ruigh-aiteachain he moved to one of the huts there. One of his paintings shows the exterior of the Duchess of Bedford's hut, with two stags' heads decorating the entrance, while a dog lies sleeping in the doorway and another peers into the hut. A Highlander lounges, apparently drowsing, against a turf-covered wall,

Inside can be seen a trunk or box, a chest of drawers, and a silver chafing dish (a heated pan for cooking) with candlesticks. There is also a glass decanter, which suggests that there were compensations for the primitive life at Ruigh-aiteachain. Mathews told how they lived on venison, grouse, hares, partridges, blackcock, ptarmigan, plovers, salmon, char, pike, trout, beef, mutton and pork.

Although the Glen Feshie sportsmen were happy roughing it in this out-of-the-way corner of the Highlands, another Landseer sketch shows that they never abandoned all the social graces. In it, the Duchess is receiving guests at a reception in one of the tents, with a piper playing at the entrance. "It is without any exception the most delightful sort of life I have ever seen or experienced," Mathews wrote in a letter to his mother. "Amusements of every sort are constantly going on. The guitar is in great request, and a small piano of two octaves, made on purpose for travelling, is constantly going."

On the other side of the Feshie, about a quarter of a mile from the main settlement, a hut originally built by the Duchess and known as the Wooden House was occupied by Horatio Ross. Mathews and other members of the main party crossed the swollen Feshie in a tilt-cart and ponies to dine with Ross. They took a tent with them as a "banqueting hall" – and carried their own knives and forks. A piper and six ghillies met them on the other side of the river and escorted them to the Wooden House.

Here again they had a mouth-watering menu – "venison in every shape and disguise, wild game and fish of every description, ending with cranberry and blueberry tarts, and all sorts of clotted cream, custards, apple-puddings and turnip-pies". The ladies retired and the men drank mulled claret and whisky toddy by a huge bonfire. After the meal, Horatio Ross, an impressive figure in a "Scotch bonnet, large smuggler's jacket, bare legs and tartan hose", led them to the river riding a large black charger.

When the Ruigh-aiteachain adventurers held a ball they invited their Glen Feshie neighbours – about a dozen in all, some living ten or twelve miles from the encampment. "Two fiddlers and a piper worked away from eight in the evening till six in the morning, when the delicate young ladies, who had walked ten miles to the ball in the rain, and waded through three fords on their way, set out again, after dancing all night, to walk back – through the three fords – ten miles to their work." A lot of whisky was drunk during the all-night festivities, but, said Mathews, "there was no one *very* fou".

It was around this time that Horatio Ross had a surprise visit from a friend, Charles Bennet, the Earl of Tankerville, one of the largest landowners in the Border area, who had an ancestral castle at Chillingham. The Earl, who had been shooting on the Duke of Atholl's estate, took a "short cut" from Atholl to Glen Feshie – up Glen Bruar and over the old Minigaig Pass; the "Miniceck", he called it. Monadh Miongaig – the "wild Month and hills of Myngegg" – was used as a route over the Grampians as far back as the sixteenth century. It was the way the drovers came from the Spey, by Ruthven and Glen Tromie.

Old maps show the Minigaig as a "Summer Road to Ruthven" and a "Foot Road to Blair of Atholl". When I crossed this ancient path a few years ago there were places where the track was hard to follow. The Earl of Tankerville, writing about his trek across the hills to Glen Feshie, said that, with peat bogs on all sides, "wayfarers and cattle had to pick their way where best they could, so all trace of the path was lost". His party came upon a man who had died in the pass only the night before.

The Earl arrived at Glen Feshie at three o'clock in the morning to find Horatio Ross casting bullets for a dawn deer hunt. The next day, he tried his luck with a forester, Charlie Mackintosh, and when they heard the crack of a gun they thought they had come upon a poacher. Charlie, who had been a poacher himself, tracked down the intruder and found "a little, strongly-built man" gralloching a deer. Then, to their surprise, this "pocket Hercules" squatted down on a stone and took out a sketchbook. The "poacher" was Edwin Landseer.

The next day, the Earl was invited over to the main settlement to join the Duke and Duchess of Bedford at lunch. He found the old Duke sitting with an umbrella over his head to prevent his soup from being watered down by a dribble from the leaking roof. He was, said the Earl, "quite happy and resigned to his fate – a wet seat in a wooden cabin instead of Woburn Abbey!"

Among Landseer's paintings from his Glen Feshie days are two oils of Loch Avon, both dated 1833. One, entitled *Lake Scene: Effect of a Storm*, looks across Loch Avon to the dark mass of the Shelter Stone Crag, with shafts of light breaking through a stormy sky. The other painting is called *Encampment on Loch Avon*. Low cloud drifts over the hills at the head of the loch. Tents have been pitched – a large one near the rocks at the foot of the Shelter Stone – and ponies graze at the water's edge. Smoke rises lazily from a fire where a group of people have gathered.

Here, Landseer has put on record scenes from an expedition which the Feshie sportsmen, including the Earl of Tankerville, made from Ruigh-aiteachain to Loch Avon. Five ponies were provided for the Duchess of Bedford, her two daughters, and two friends. The men were on foot. Charles Mathews, a Londoner, appeared in a smart kilt, complete with dirk and sporran, drawing some odd looks from sceptical ghillies.

That night, grouped around the fire, they sang Scots ballads and listened to Mathews'

Ponies graze today on the green flats by the Feshie at Ruigh-aiteachain, described by Queen Victoria as "the scene of all Landseer's glory".

version of a song called "Jinnie Jones". When it was over, the men left the women in their tents and, lighting a lantern, crossed the slippery boulders to the Poacher's Cave. There is little doubt that this was the Shelter Stone cave, but it was less well-known then. One of the foresters pointed it out to them. Next morning they were on their way back to Glen Feshie – and the end of the Earl of Tankerville's holiday. "It was a sad moment when we saw the last of Glenfeshie," he said.

Sixty years later, Lt. Gen. Henry Hope Crealock, whose book, *Deerstalking in the Highlands of Scotland*, was published in 1892, travelled through Glen Feshie and noted that the Duchess of Bedford's bothy was "in sad ruin". In the hut which was used as a dining room there was a large drawing of deer, a "charming sketch", said the General. Knowing that it was probably doomed to destruction, he got a sheet of drawing paper and made a careful copy of it. There was also a building known as Landseer's Hut. In 1929, when John A. Gavin, a member of the Cairngorm Club, was at Ruigh-aiteachain,

Bothy at Ruigh-aiteachain.

it was beginning to fall to pieces, but part of a deer fresco over the fireplace could still be seen. Like Gen. Crealock, Gavin took a tracing of the deer's head and drew a sketch of the interior of the hut.

Now, apart from the gable-end of the hut where Edwin Landseer is said to have stayed, there is nothing left to recall those idyllic days when the Duchess of Bedford held court at Ruigh-aiteachain, When I was in Glen Feshie, I discovered that others had been chasing Landseer's ghost. Mrs Lorna Dempster, wife of Alec Dempster, head stalker on the Glen Feshie estate, lives in a house overlooking the Ruigh-aiteachain – "The Huts" – and is often asked about the painter.

She told me about the oddest visitor she had ever seen, a man she met on the Feshie track. He was wearing a soft hat, a long coat, a rolled umbrella, and carrying a briefcase. "He looked a proper city gent," said Mrs Dempster. He said he was a descendant of the famous painter. Inside his briefcase were a number of Landseer's sketches, and he had apparently come to the glen to match the drawings to the landscape. She never discovered who he was; it was another mysterious tailpiece to the Landseer story.

Today, life has come back to the glen in a different way. Not far from the fragment of Landseer's bothy there is a hostel for climbers and hill-walkers. Here, they sit around the fire and swap stories just as "Lanny" and his companions did all those years ago. But I was thinking of another person when I stood at Ruigh-aiteachain, watching ponies graze on the green flats by the Feshie.

It is 130 years since Queen Victoria came riding through the glen on the back of a pony, Brown wading through the Eidart holding its head. They had come this way the previous year on their way to Speyside and had stopped at Ruigh-aiteachain – "the scene of all Landseer's glory", said Victoria. This time, on the opposite side of the river, they stopped again to look at the site of the old encampment. "The huts, surrounded by magnificent fir trees, and by quantities of juniper bushes, looked lovelier than ever," the Queen wrote in her *Journal*. "We gazed with sorrow at their utter ruin."

CHAPTER 8

PAINTERS
IN THE
HEATHER

BUFFALO ONCE ROAMED THE SLOPES OF BIRNAM HILL. They were brought from the plains of America by Sir William Drummond Stewart, 7th Baronet of Murthly and 19th Lord of Grandtully, soldier, explorer, hunter, author and businessman. When he died in 1871, the buffalo continued to terrorise the neighbourhood for many years, but they were gradually killed off. Now only the deer run wild on Buffalo Hill.

This adventurous Highland laird never did things by half. When his son George took part in the Charge of the Light Brigade and was awarded the Victoria Cross, his father welcomed him home by building a giant arch and calling it the Malakoff Arch after one of the Crimean battles.

Today, like Shakespeare's tale of Birnam woods, Sir William's exploits – and his buffalo – have slipped into local lore, but down in Birnam there is another, more permanent reminder of Murthly extravagance. This is the gateway that rises in gargantuan splendour at one end of the Birnam Hotel, which, with its enormous baronial hall, has itself come in for some awed comment.

Through this huge gate a three-mile drive led to Murthly Castle. Along the drive were ornate and elegant villas taken over by sportsmen during the shooting season. Some can still be seen today. Two were rented by the painter John Everett Millais, a man who, like his friend Landseer, came to Scotland with a gun in one hand and a paintbrush in the other.

Millais rented the Murthly shooting for twelve years. The Laird of Murthly's buffaloes had probably gone by then, or been drastically thinned out, but the painter had plenty of other wildlife to keep him busy. He would sit in "the Bog", a strip of land in the middle of one of the grouse moors, and watch the duck, teal and snipe rise in a great rush of sound when the guns opened up. It was said that when the first shot of the season was fired a thousand ducks and teal rose into the air.

He was also a fishing enthusiast. He had a beat specially reserved for himself on the River Tay, looking up towards Birnam from the Stenton bank, where he often stopped for a picnic lunch after fishing. It was from there that he painted his landscape, *Murthly Water* in 1888. That same autumn he painted *The Old Garden*, showing the garden of the old castle at Murthly. It brought a poetic comment from George de Maurier about the garden's "old-world grace".

Millais, who also fancied himself as a poet (he once won £10 in a Burns competition), decided to send de Maurier some game. He wrote a letter which began:

My dear, dear George,
If you would gorge
Pheasants, hares and partridges,
Just tell me where
To send, mon cher,
The victims of my cartridges.

His son, J. G. Millais, himself an accomplished painter of game birds, once related how his father "used to squat behind his favourite whin bush, banging away to left and right and occasionally fetching down what he persisted in calling 'the teal that at heaven's gate sings'." The victims of his cartridges were not always feathered. He took a shot at a partridge while passing a cottage in a turnip field. His shot killed the bird, peppered an old woman sitting knitting at her window, and smashed five panes of glass.

Both Millais and Landseer were said to be torn between gun and brush. There is a story, probably apocryphal, that when a blackcock flew over Millais while he was painting he dropped his palette, grabbed his gun, shot the bird, and then went back to his painting.

While Millais was crouching in his whin bush in "the Bog", other artists were heading north with brush or gun, and sometimes with both. The artist-hunter was a familiar figure last century. The great William Scrope dabbled in landscape art and was said by Sir Walter Scott to be "one of the very best amateur painters" he had ever seen. He drew or painted landscapes for the pictures in his own books and got friends like Edwin and Charles Landseer to fill in the deer and the dogs.

Landseer was one of the first of the Victorian artists to make the Scottish moors his stamping ground last century, and a long line of artists fell in line behind him. Richard Ansdell was close on his heels; so close, in fact, that he was accused of imitation. One critic said that if there had been no Landseer, Ansdell would have held "the very foremost place in this department of art". Another of Landseer's contemporaries, Frederick Taylor, spotted an engraving of one of his works, *Weighing the Deer*, in a shop window and was annoyed to see it described as a "beautiful engraving from the original by Sir Edwin Landseer".

Prince Albert was interested in both sketching and shooting, but he was a poor marksman and an indifferent draughtsman. He liked etching – Queen Victoria wrote

A drawing entitled *Deerstalking*, by William Scrope and Edwin Landseer. Scrope often drew or painted landscapes and got friends to fill in other details. Courtesy of National Galleries of Scotland.

about how the two of them passed the time "singing after breakfast and etching together". As for his hunting, *Punch* magazine took a xenophobic delight in telling its readers that he was an appallingly bad shot.

He was no more successful at fishing. He tried his hand at leistering – spearing salmon. This type of fishing was a kind of Tinchel on water, with an army of ghillies driving the fish towards the waiting fishermen. Queen Victoria wrote about leistering in her *Journal* in September, 1850. "It had a very pretty effect," she said, "about one hundred men wading through the river, some in kilts with poles and spears, all very much excited." The excitement reached fever pitch – "a great fright", said the Queen – when two non-swimmers waded into a deep pool and got into difficulties. They were rescued by Dr Andrew Robertson, the Balmoral factor.

The leistering went on. "We were very successful," reported Victoria, "seven salmon being caught, some in the net and some speared." She added cryptically, "Though Albert stood in the water some time he caught nothing." Victoria thought the scene "exciting and picturesque" and wished that Landseer was there to sketch it. She drew it herself, one of her few attempts at a group scene. Three years later, however, another Royal artist was there to capture the excitement of leistering.

That was in 1853, when anyone standing on the banks of the River Dee at Balmoral would have seen Prince Albert's Jagar, John Macdonald, plunge into the river and, up to his waist in water, go splashing across the river with a man on his back. His "passenger" was the artist Carl Haag, who had been spotted by Queen Victoria from the opposite side of the river and summoned to the Royal presence. The Queen wanted to give him advice on the sketches he was doing of the salmon-spearing.

While the beaters banged their poles to drive the fish towards the waiting nets, Albert and his two eldest sons stood on rocks jabbing their three-pronged spears at the salmon as they passed. This time the Prince was lucky, spearing three fish. Later, the Queen asked Haag to paint a "secret picture" of the leistering as a birthday present for Albert. It was to show John Macdonald in the water with the Prince of Wales and Prince Alfred.

The Queen thought that Macdonald was "remarkably tall and handsome". He appeared in a number of Royal sketches. The Prince Consort sketched him lying in the heather watching for deer, and he also featured prominently in the Landseer painting, *Royal Sports on Hill and Loch*. The Queen, always meticulous about the grouping of the paintings she commissioned, said it would show her stepping out of the boat at Loch Muick, Albert – "in his Highland dress" – assisting her. "I am looking at the stag which he is supposed to have just killed. Bertie is on the deer pony with Macdonald (whom Landseer much admires) standing behind with rifles and plaids on his shoulder."

Victoria wanted the painting to be "singularly dignified, poetical and totally novel". Landseer's initial sketch showed Macdonald with a rifle over his shoulder, but in the finished work he is seen holding a fish. This was to show that the Queen had been fishing while Albert was shooting, but there was nothing dignified or poetical about the bearded ghillie holding up a dead fish. Landseer started the painting in 1850 and was still messing about with it, making changes, twenty years later. When he saw it on the walls of the Royal Academy in 1870, he shuddered.

The first sketch had one stag in it, but by the time it was finished another had been added. No painting was complete without a corpse or two. Carl Haag's first major commission in 1854, *Evening at Balmoral* or *Showing the Stags by Torch*, began to take shape when he was called to Balmoral Castle at nine o'clock to join the Royal party at the main entrance. They were there to see the stags that Prince Albert had killed that day – a "showing" carried out by torchlight.

Two nights later, the scene was re-enacted, Colonel C. Gordon, the Prince's Equerry, helping Haag to arrange the stags and torch-bearers so that he could plan his composition. The painting shows two stags lying in front of the Queen and her elegantly-dressed guests, while the Prince, in full Highland dress, has one hand on his hip and the other on the tip of a dead stag's antler. To complete this gory re-enactment a third stag was slung over the back of a pony.

The stag–pony formula was repeated in *Queen Victoria Sketching at Loch Laggan*, which was the first of Landseer's pictures of the Royal family in the Highlands. He described the scene in a letter to a friend: ". . . forester with deer hounds, pony, deer on his back &cc. The Q. and P. Albert are quite mad about it." Despite the painting's deceptive informality, it is clear that the characters in it have been carefully placed.

The Loch Laggan picture paved the way for *Royal Sports* – and it, in turn, acted as a signpost to the future. *Royal Sports*, as Queen Victoria said, was "totally novel". She saw it as "a new conception", vastly different from the stilted art of the court portrait. "It will tell a great deal," she said. What, in fact, it told, or foretold, was that the Queen would use art as a medium of Royal record. With a string of artists working to her instructions, she created the visual equivalent of her *Highland Journals*.

Albert and Victoria began to make what they called "souvenir albums" shortly after their marriage, and over a period of twenty years filled nine volumes with over 600 watercolours, including more than 100 Scottish views. The ninth volume, completed a month before the death of Prince Albert, contained pictures of the Royal couple's last Great Expeditions from Balmoral.

Hundreds of Queen Victoria's drawings and watercolours are in the Royal Collection at Windsor, taking their place alongside pictures painted for the souvenir albums by professional artists. One of her early instructors was William Leighton Leitch, a Glasgow man, who made a living by decorating snuff boxes. "Good old Leitch" the Queen called him. He stayed with her for nearly twenty years.

Leitch, in a letter to his wife, described one of his outdoor painting sessions with the Queen: . . . "her Majesty sitting in the middle of a country road, with a great rough stone out of the river to put her paint box on; Lady Churchill holding an umbrella over the Queen's head, and I seated near her Majesty so that she could see what I was doing." Nearby was a servant Leitch called "the Highlander". His name was John Brown.

Lady Charlotte Canning, who was the Queen's Lady-in-Waiting at Blair and Balmoral in 1848, 1852, 1853 and 1855, was also one of Leitch's students. Among the paintings Leitch and his pupil produced – the "pretty views" the Queen wanted for her souvenir albums – were watercolours of Glen Tilt, the long pass that runs from Blair to Deeside, linking up with the formidable Lairig Ghru. Six of Leitch's watercolours and six of Lady Canning's were given a place in the albums.

Another contributor to the Royal souvenir albums was a young artist called William Henry Fisk, who painted four watercolours for them. Victoria thought that he was one of a number of artists who owed their success to Prince Albert's interest in their work, but it may be that Fisk's romantic gesture at Crathie Church had something to do with his success. Fisk was there when the Queen came out of the kirk in pouring rain. He took off his plaid and in a sweeping Sir Walter Raleigh gesture spread it in front of the Queen so that she could walk to her carriage without getting her feet wet.

Not surprisingly, James Giles featured prominently in the line-up of Royal painters. He was the Aberdeen artist whose sketches helped to persuade Victoria that Balmoral should be her Scottish home. It was Giles who helped Prince Albert to set up a Balmoral School of Art, where young men were taught furniture-making and young women were taught embroidery.

A portrait of William Leighton Leitch by E.J. Bridell-Fox. Leitch was a Glasgow man who was one of Queen Victoria's favourite instructors in the arts of drawing and painting. Courtesy of National Galleries of Scotland.

The Aberdeen photographer, George Washington Wilson, who was himself a painter before discarding his brush for a lens, also helped to build up a record of the Queen's travels. Victoria frequently commissioned him to photograph specific scenes, some in advance of her trips, others *after* them. This sort of post-dated approach applied to painting as well as photography. In 1861, when she wanted to recapture the excitement of some of her earlier expeditions, she sent Washington Wilson off to take a number of views of the glens she had ridden through. Not satisfied with this, she then enlisted the help of William Leitch's son, Richard. "The younger Leitch has been to Blair to make Sketches of our dear, dear Expeditions and is going to make all the remaining views where I can never photograph", she wrote to Princess Alice.

The kind of patronage handed out by Queen Victoria virtually ended with her death. Painting in the heather also became a thing of the past, nudged into the background by the developing art of photography. Now the groupings were done for the camera ... the Prince of Wales (later King Edward VII) at an *al fresco* lunch on the moors, or with his house-guests outside Derry Lodge in Mar Forest; King George V, also as Prince of Wales, riding to the butts in the early 1900s; and yet another future king, George VI, picnicking during a shoot near Balmoral in 1933.

But the old sporting paintings and prints remained very much in demand. A late nineteenth-century painting, *Grouse Shooting on the Glentanar Estate*, an oil on canvas by Carl Suhrlandt, was sold by Christie's Scotland in Edinburgh in 1988 for £16,500. Signed and dated 1889, it shows Sir William Cunliffe Brooks, the Laird of Glentanar, with Charles Gordon, 11th Marquis of Huntly, out on the Deeside moors. In the picture is a noted stalker, Donald McIntosh.

Nor is that rare breed, the hunter-artist, totally extinct. Roger McPhail, who is said to be as much at home with a gun as a paintbrush, is one of the leading grouse moor painters. His evocative *Grouse Driving in Aberdeenshire*, painted in 1977, is set against a spreading panorama of North-east farmland, with grouse shooters firing from butts on a hill. McPhail's skill as a bird painter is appreciated by thousands of people, although many of them have no interest in either art or wildlife. They are whisky-drinkers with a taste for Grouse. The bird on the front of the bottle was painted by Roger McPhail.

Of course, not all his birds are on whisky bottles. Howard Butterworth, the Deeside painter, showed me a small and delicate McPhail bird painting which he has in his possession. Howard, who has himself built up a considerable reputation in the last dozen or so years, is an artist who not only paints the glens, but lives and works in one – a Royal glen. He is not a "hunting" artist, but he has covered the sport in some of his paintings. He has sold his pictures to a Royal neighbour, the Queen Mother, whose house at Birkhall, across the River Muick, is less than half a mile away.

Howard's home and studio at Croft Cottage is on a hillock not far from the ford

Howard Butterworth, the Deeside painter, at work on location by the roadside.

which Queen Victoria crossed on her way to her "little bothie" at Allt-na Guibhsaich. It has become known to hundreds of visitors to Glenmuick by the sign at the roadside, "Paintings and Pullovers". The pullovers are the work of Howard's wife Hilary, who took me into two small caravans which serve as makeshift exhibition centres. Inside, the paintings included one of Aucholzie (pronounced Achwylie), a croft farther up the glen.

When I was there, snow had fallen over the hills. Lochnagar was grey and threatening. Looking at it, I thought of Butterworth's painting, *Melting Snow on Lochnagar*, which shows the Muick winding through a heathery landscape, with the distant mountain cold and aloof, streaked with white. Down at the Crofts farm, watching sheep foraging for food in the snow-covered fields, I was reminded of another painting, a scene from a canvas by Joseph Farquharson, the Laird of Finzean, whose fondness for snow scenes with sheep in them won him the nickname of "Frozen Mutton".

I found Howard behind the farm buildings at the Crofts farm, wrapped up against the bitter cold. The canvas on his easel showed a flock of sheep being driven home through the snow, so he was "doing a Farquharson". He might resent that sort of comparison, for he is very much his own man, with his own ideas, his own style, and his own ambitions as a painter. I discovered that the tiny figure in the painting was Ron Cowie, the Crofts farmer. He had seen it, unfinished, and had said it was "going to be a cracker".

Howard and his wife Hilary are, both from Rochdale and have been in Glenmuick for fourteen years. He was not drawn there by the Royal tag, and it is obvious that he is not particularly animated by the thought of Royalty on his doorstep. The only member of the Royal family he has met is the Queen Mother, who visited him at Crofts Cottage and bought his *Scarlet Poppies in Glenmuick* and *Almond Trees in Blossom*. His paintings are rich with the colours of Deeside's changing seasons. When he started selling them in Aberdeen they were fetching anything from £17 to £25; now their value is measured in thousands of pounds. One of his canvasses sold for £3,750.

Hanging on a wall in my home is an icily impressive painting of Lochnagar in winter, seen from the Meikle Pap, with the dark scar of the Black Gully set against one of those grey, shivering skies that you get in the hills at year-end. The artist was Eric Auld, an Aberdeen man, who has painted more Deeside glens than any other painter I know. Loch Muick and the glen itself have both come under his brush, as well as glens that are less well-known, like Callater, beyond Braemar, which stretches away to the Tolmounth and the windy heights of Jock's Road.

Lately, he has been exploring the little glens. I remember the first time I saw the name Camlet in Glen Girnock. I thought at first that is was Camelot and that I was caught up in Arthurian fantasy, but the name comes from *cam lichd*, and, more prosaically, means "bent hillside". The farm is actually on a curious bend in the hill, like a corrie, and up behind its ruined farm buildings I found the wreck of an old car. I discovered recently that Eric had put this desolate scene, including the car, on canvas.

It is out on these Deeside moors and hills that another painter gets his inspiration. Willie Forbes, formerly head stalker on the Mar Lodge estate, is one of Scotland's leading taxidermists – they called them "stuffers" in the old days. By an odd coincidence, his home at Corriemulzie, a few miles west of Braemar, was built a century ago by the noted Deeside taxidermist John Lamont.

Willie has built up a considerable reputation as both a taxidermist and a painter. He was on a "shoot" on one occasion when he was given a lift by a member of the party. "You're the stuffer, aren't you?" said the man at the wheel. His driver was the Duke of Edinburgh.

Willie has done a number of stags' heads for the Duke. When I saw him at Corriemulzie he was working on exhibits which were to be on show to the public at Balmoral Castle. They were different from the kind of taxidermy he did a few years ago. Now, instead of simply sticking a bird or an animal on a plinth, he recreates its natural habitat, setting it against a background of rocks and heather.

This has to do with environmental issues. People are much more conservation-minded, he says, and as attitudes have changed, his technique has had to change. Inside his workshop were lifelike groupings of animals and their prey, among them an otter

Eric Auld, an Aberdeen man, is well known for his paintings of Deeside glens. One of his works incorporates this desolate scene, with car.

clutching a salmon and a fox about to pounce on a rabbit.

He is an accomplished painter. Over his fireplace at Corriemulzie is a Victorian print of a stalker in a tartan "tammie", sitting with his dog beside the huge antlered head of a dead stag. Willie jokes about it, saying that if he had gone back with a stag head like that when he was a keeper *he* would have been shot. Yet he is one of the few contemporary painters who still follow the Victorian tradition of painting stalking scenes. One of his early works, *The Drookit*, showing a dead hummel stag being taken off the hill on the back of a pony, has been reproduced in 2,500 prints.

There is no English word that has the same squelching impact as "drookit" … drenched, soaked, sodden, dripping with water – DROOKIT. That is how it is in Willie's painting. Rain slants down over the hills and a drenched ponyman splashes through a stream without even bothering to look for stepping stones.

Willie once told me that watching a dead stag going down the glen in a machine gave him no satisfaction at the end of the day. What *did* give him satisfaction was seeing it being taken off the hill the traditional way, as it had been done for the past hundred years at Mar Lodge, with the stalker following the old pony paths, crossing burns, finding his way back to the nearest road and a waiting Land Rover.

Today, not everybody wants a painting simply as a record of a "kill". He showed me a picture of a roe buck on the edge of a wood, dawn breaking through the trees behind it. It had been caught at the instant when, suddenly on the alert, it had turned to look at the hunter – and then it vanished. It was that frozen moment in time that remained in the hunter's mind – and that was what he wanted Willie to put on canvas for him.

Another of his works, *The Crossing*, illustrates the trouble he will go to to ensure that he has the right setting for his pictures. *The Crossing* was commissioned by Sir Seton Wills, of the Inchrory estate at Tomintoul, after Lady Wills had shot an old stag

Willie Forbes, formerly head stalker on the Mar Lodge Estate, has built up a reputation as a painter and a taxidermist. Here he is seen with the head of a fox which he stalked after spotting it from the window of his house a few miles from Braemar.

– a "Royal". He undertook to have the head "stuffed" – "prepared" is how the taxidermist describes it – but Lady Wills also wanted the stag painted, with a background that was recognisably Inchrory. Willie set off with a sketchbook and camera, and the result was a striking painting of a herd of deer crossing over the river above Inchrory Lodge – led by Lady Wills's "Royal".

"At some time or another stags from all the estates around here will end up in this little studio", said Willie. It won't simply be so that another stag's head can be stuck up on the wall. That's what happened in the past; there are, for instance, over 3,000 heads in the hall at Mar Lodge, and stags' heads and antlers pack the roof and walls of the ballroom at Glentanar, each with an inscription noting who shot it and when.

Nowadays, it is just as likely that the deer to be stuffed has died of old age, a veteran that, as Willie put it...has "done his bit for the hill", and that the laird wants the head "prepared" or a painting made of it because the dead animal represents the quality of stock on the estate.

Deer on the moors, a salmon leaping from the river, grouse rising from the heather...Willie Forbes sees it all and tucks it away in his mind to bring alive again through his paintings and taxidermy. Like Landseer in Glenfeshie and Millais in the Bog at Murthly, he finds fulfilment with both gun and paintbrush. "The need to get out and about is sometimes very overpowering," he told me. "I have to go to the hills shooting and fishing to get inspiration and to freshen my mind up for painting."

CHAPTER 9

FIDDLER

AND

STALKER

THE SOUND OF THE FIDDLE floated over the trim streets and tidy gardens of Little Dunkeld, dancing a reel around the weatherbeaten stones in the ancient churchyard. It could have been old Bob Horne's bow that was playing a tune, for this local fiddler's house is no more than a couple of streets away from the kirkyard. On the other hand, it might have been a trick of the imagination, for at the time I was thinking of the great days of fiddling in Atholl.

I had gone to Little Dunkeld to see where Niel Gow, the man they called the King of Rant and Reel, was buried. Gow's fiddle playing won him a place among the musical immortals, and when he died in 1807 some anonymous rhymester wrote:

Gow and Time are equal now;
Gow beat time, now Time's beat Gow.

In some ways, he was buried in the wrong place. He should have been laid to rest in the village of Inver, across the River Tay, for that was where he was born (or, at any rate, at Strathbraan, just up the river) and that was where they came to listen to the music from his dancing bow.

Inver has been swept aside by the remorseless tide of traffic that separates it from Dunkeld. Before the building of a bridge over the Tay, when there were three ferries plying across the river, it was the connection for the West Ferry. It was at the inn there that travellers stopped for a night on their way north. Now it is a forgotten backwater, a sleepy little community where the old road no longer goes anywhere, beating itself out against the high banks of the A9.

This corner of Atholl is haunted by the sound of the fiddle, for half the fiddlers in Scotland seem to have lived in the area, or played there. The inn at Inver, where they paid court to Niel Gow, no longer exists, but whitewashed houses still cluster around its

The inn at Inver no longer exists, but the whitewashed houses still cluster around its courtyard.

courtyard. Nearby, a wooden seat stands in front of a tall tree, which has a faded noticeboard nailed to it. There are no notices on it – Inver, it seems, has little to tell the world these days.

Yet what tales it *could* tell. Gow, who played before Bonnie Prince Charlie (he made the symbolic gesture of following the Prince on his march south as far as Stirling), was a friend of poets like James Hogg, the Ettrick Shepherd, Lady Nairne and Robert Burns. The Atholl fiddler played at dances and assemblies for more than forty years. He was so popular that when he was ill the Caledonian Hunt Ball was postponed until he was well enough to play at it. Lady Nairne's sister told of another ball that became a disaster when Niel was held up by the weather – "the storm froze up the company as well as Niel Gow".

The fiddler who stood in for Gow was disparagingly called "a scraper". Burns described himself as " a fiddler and a poet", but he was also a bit of a scraper, for his fiddling was a lot less noticeable than his poetry. He called his fellow-fiddlers "brother catguts", and when he stayed at Dunkeld during his tour of Scotland he went to see Gow at his cottage at Inver. Gow played a number of airs for him and afterwards they adjourned to the inn for a farewell drink.

Niel Gow, violinist and composer, with his brother Nathaniel, after David Allan. Courtesy of National Galleries of Scotland.

Gow liked his dram, but he was never a heavy drinker, and a row erupted after he had composed a tune called "Farewell to Whisky", which was about the banning of whisky-making in 1799 after a disastrous harvest. Mrs Agnes Lyon, the wife of a Glamis minister, followed it up with an innocent poem entitled "Niel Gow's Farewell to Whisky":

> You've surely heard of famous Niel,
> The man who played the fiddle weel;
> He was a heartsome, merry chiel,
> And weel he lo'ed the whisky, O!
> For e'er since he wore the tartan hose
> He dearly liket Athole brose!
> And grieved was, you may suppose,
> To bid "Farewell to whisky", O!

One writer, P.R. Drummond, attacked the minister's wife for giving the impression that Niel Gow "was a devout worshipper of Bacchus". Mrs Lyon committed an even worse sin. Her spelling of the great man's Christian name was wrong – or right, depending on how you look at it. She gave it as Neil. Gow himself chose to spell his name the "wrong" way.

Elizabeth Grant, in her *Memoirs of a Highland Lady*, recalled hearing Gow play at Inver inn in 1804, when she was a child of seven. He was in his late 70s then, and she could never have foreseen that eighteen years later, when she was sending Glenlivet whisky to George IV in Edinburgh, Gow's son, Nathaniel, would be in Auld Reekie playing the fiddle for the king.

In 1815, Elizabeth made another stop on her way north to Rothiemurchus. "The scenery is exquisite," she wrote, "every step leads to new beauties, and after the wanderings of the morning it was but a pleasure to return to the quiet inn at Inver to dine and rest and have Niel Gow in the evening to play the violin. It was the last time we were there; the next time we travelled the road the new bridge over the Tay at Dunkeld was finished, the new inn, the Duke's Arms, opened, the ferry and the inn at Inver done up, and Niel Gow was dead."

Gow, a weaver's son, owed a great deal to the 3rd Duke of Atholl, who acted as his sponsor, paying him a retainer of £5 a year. When the Duke and his family went off to London for the "season", they took "the Scotch fiddler" with them to play at their *soirées*. Later, the Atholl family gave the same sponsorship to Niel's son, Nathaniel, who became no less famous than his father.

Nathaniel's band – Gow's Celebrated Band – was a roaring success with Royal Geordie, who was himself "a respectable violencello player". After listening to them play in Edinburgh, he gave instructions that some of his precious Glenlivet whisky should be used to make Athole Brose for the band. The emphasis was on the whisky, less on the oatmeal and honey, and Nathaniel's fiddlers went merrily home playing "I'll ay ca' by in yon town".

When I went from Little Dunkeld to Inver, crossing the busy A9, I wondered what

Gow would have thought about the traffic-ridden highway that today carries travellers north to Inverness and south to Perth. More than two centuries ago, he saw what was then the new road from Dunkeld to Perth, paid for by the Duke of Atholl.

The poet Robert Southey mentioned this "good road" during his tour of Scotland in 1819 and recalled Gow's reaction when the fiddler heard someone praising it in front of the Duke. Niel said they could boast about their roads if they wanted to, but when he had "a wee droppie" at Perth it took him "just as lang gettin' hame by the new road as by the aul' een". Southey said that Gow took "a zig-zag course, tacking always from one side of it to the other". So much for his farewell to whisky!

Going down into Inver is like wandering into the tranquil world that Niel Gow knew, yet there is virtually nothing there to indicate that it was the home of the great fiddler. The cottage he lived in hides away in a lane that once ran on to the north road, but now comes to an abrupt halt under the A9. The cottage has its back to the lane, as if turning away from inquisitive visitors, and in the window of the kitchen there is, or was, a piece of cardboard with the words "Niel Gow Cottage". Beside it another card advertises "Bed and Breakfast".

On this back wall, half-hidden behind a hedge and difficult to read, there is an unimpressive black plaque in memory of Niel, his son Nathaniel, and his grandson

Niel Gow's cottage.

Niel, jun., who was also a fiddler. The front of the house is more attractive, with flowers and a neatly-kept lawn running down to the waters of the Braan, but I imagine that many people visit the village without even discovering where Gow lived – or even knowing that he lived there at all.

Up in Blair Castle, a portrait of the famous fiddler gazes down on the thousands of visitors who wander through its stately corridors. The present Duke of Atholl has kept faith with the Gow tradition, for the castle has housed some of the fiddlers' rallies that are all the rage nowadays. But in Dunkeld, steeped in history and crowded with tourists, you could look in vain for anything to show that people once came from far and wide to listen to the magic bow of the Atholl weaver's son.

There is a curious irony in the fact that the only man in the Dunkeld and District Strathspey and Reel Society is an 83-year-old fiddler from Buchan – a man who regards James Scott Skinner as his hero, not Niel Gow. It may be a dangerous, almost sacrilegious thing to say in Atholl, but Bob Horne, who lives near Gow's burial place, thinks that Skinner was a higher class of fiddler. But Gow, he accepts, was the Master.

Bob would admit to being a "scraper". He learned to play the fiddle at his home at New Pitsligo in the days when a lot of people "scrapit an' scratchit" and were happy if they could produce a tune. He played at different events in the North-east. He would put his fiddle into a wooden box, tie it with string, sling it over his shoulder, and go off on his bike to entertain the fiddle-daft folk of Buchan.

He still goes out and about with his fiddle. When I saw him in Dunkeld he was preparing to leave the next day for a fiddlers' rally in Elgin. There are about twenty-five members in the Strathspey and Reel Society and Bob is the oldest, as well as being the only one from Dunkeld. The others come from places like Pitlochry, Bankfoot and Perth.

In Niel Gow's day they could have formed half a dozen strathspey and reel societies. Inver was famous for its fiddlers and Niel Gow himself produced a crop of them – four sons, William, John, Andrew and Nathaniel, who were all involved in music. Nathaniel and John had a music-publishing business. A fifth son, Daniel, died in infancy. Niel's brother, Donald, accompanied his brother when he played at dances and assemblies, vamping on the "bass" fiddle, or cello. After his death, his place was taken by Malcolm McDonald, and later by Patrick Murray, both Inver men.

Gow was often invited to play before the Duke of Atholl and other prominent figures in Perthshire's high society, but not all the local lairds were mere listeners. General William Robertson of Lude, whose clashes with his neighbour at Blair Castle were well-known, was himself a fiddle-player. In 1779, one of the Duke of Atholl's relatives, Mary Murray, went to tea at General Robertson's in London and noted that "the Scotch Fiddler appeared".

Niel Gow's cottage housed another fiddler. After his death it was occupied by Duncan M'Kerracher, who was born in Inver and was sometimes known as the Atholl Paganini. Opposite the cottage a plaque on another house marks it out as the home of Charles MacIntosh, a post runner (postman) who walked thirty miles a day carrying the mail. He was a talented musician, a 'cellist in his brother's string band, but it was as a self-taught naturalist that he made a name for himself, becoming widely respected as an authority on the subject.

Beatrix Potter, the children's writer and illustrator, was one of his great admirers. She came to Scotland in 1871 at the age of five, living at Dalguise House, north of Inver. It became her holiday home for the next ten years. In 1892 she returned to Heath Park, near Birnam Station, and in 1893 stayed at Eastwood, downstream from the Dunkeld Bridge.

It was in 1892 that she wrote in her *Journal* of her attempts to meet Charles MacIntosh – "trying all summer to speak with that shy but learned man". She eventually invited him to tea at Heath Park, discussed her drawings of fungi with him, and corresponded with him when she went back to London. When she was seventeen, she became reluctant to return to Dalguise, afraid that, with her childhood behind her, she would find that its old magic had gone. "The future is dark and uncertain," she wrote, "let me keep to the past."

There is a picture of Charles MacIntosh in *Dunkeld Remembered*, a booklet in which Mary Crerar, a well-loved figure in Dunkeld, looked back on the old days and forgotten characters in the town. He is carrying a stick and wearing a wide-brimmed trilby hat, and his long straggling white beard lies like a bird's nest over his black overcoat. He looks as if he had stepped from the pages of one of Beatrix Potter's books, like Mrs Tiggy Winkle, who was really Kitty Macdonald, the laundry maid at Dalguise.

With MacIntosh in the picture is his niece, Elizabeth MacIntosh, who was co-author of *Dunkeld Remembered*, which was produced by the Dunkeld and Birnam Historical Society. Mary, who died in 1987 in her early 80s, recalled seeing Charles MacIntosh bringing brilliantly coloured fungi to Dunkeld School for the pupils to paint.

One of Mary's forbears was John Crerar, head forester (deer stalker) on the Atholl estate. Atholl was known for both its fiddlers and its foresters, and Crerar filled both roles. Taught by Niel Gow, he composed a number of reels, mostly inspired by the Atholl glens he knew so well. Among them were "The Duke of Atholl's Forest" and "Forest Lodge". Queen Victoria, going through Glen Tilt to Deeside in 1861, went by carriage as far as Forest Lodge, eight miles from Blair, and from there by pony to Bynack.

William Scrope, in *The Art of Deer-Stalking*, told of a song which was sung every night at Forest Lodge early last century. Written by one of the Duke of Atholl's servants, it carries the verse:

> John Crerar he spies out the harts,
> My Lord Duke does shoot them;
> Curly he does bring them home,
> And Campbell he does cook them.

Curly was John Forbes, whose job was to go to the hill with two horses and bring home the dead deer. Campbell was a cook with the Atholl family for more than sixty years, working in his later years as a hill-cook.

John Crerar, who died in 1840 at the age of 90, became something of a legend. His place in Atholl history was ensured when he was painted by Landseer in *Death of a Hart in Glen Tilt*. In it he is seen with the 4th Duke of Atholl, who was once described as "the greatest deer killer in Scotland". The Duke's young grandson, George Murray, who later became the 6th Duke, is also in the painting, as is Crerar's son Charles, who is holding out a knife to the Duke before disembowelling a stag.

Crerar appeared in two other Landseer paintings, one an oil sketch for *Death of a Hart*, the other, painted in 1824, entitled *Keeper John Crerar with Pony*. The legend loses some of its sparkle in these paintings, for Crerar is seen as a balding, dumpy little man. In the main picture he has a spyglass clapped to his eye and a deerstalking hat on his head, with a powderhorn slung around his body and a rifle beside him. He is wearing a smart jacket and knee breeches.

Although correct dress was the order of the day among the hunting fraternity last century, there were occasions when the painter, striving for the right note of formality, tended to over-dress his subject. This was shown in a painting of Willie Duff, another fiddler and forester of Atholl, who was painted by the artist Kenneth MacLeay as part of a series of portraits of Highlanders commissioned by Queen Victoria in 1855.

MacLeay may have been influenced by Queen Victoria's romantic idea of what the typical Highlander looked like, or what she thought he *should* look like, for the subjects of MacLeay's portraits were strong, manly figures, kilted and plaided, immaculately dressed, fitting well into the conventional picture of the faithful Highland retainer. There were times, however, when reality and myth had little in common, and nowhere was this more evident than in the watercolour of the Atholl fisherman known as "Beardie" Willie.

In MacLeay's painting, Duff is shown as a smart, dignified kilted figure, a proud Highlander, his long white beard carefully combed, gazing steadfastly at the painter. There is, however, a contemporary photograph showing a different Duff, dishevelled and ill at ease. A rough horsehair sporran dangles from his kilt, which hangs lopsidedly over one knee, and his long hair and untidy beard frame a frowning, anxious face. Whether MacLeay worked from the photograph, or it was taken after the painting was completed, with "Beardie" holding the same pose, is unclear.

Willie is seen in MacLeay's painting alongside the military figure of Sgt. Major Duncan MacBeath, an Atholl Highlander. He himself was in the Atholl Highlanders – "playing soldiers", is how Lady Canning, Queen Victoria's Lady-in-Waiting, described it. In those days he was called Billy Duff and was painted by Charles Landseer, Edwin's brother. Lady Canning described him as "a savage picturesque keeper with a long black beard".

When he went to the Eglinton Tournament with Lord Glenlyon, he made three attempts to get out of camp by sneaking past the sentries. He was caught and kept prisoner in his tent all night and next morning was given bread and water for breakfast as punishment. "Beardie", whose picture once hung in the Hermitage at Inver (it was later removed to Blair Castle) not only played the fiddle and sang, but tied salmon flies and knitted elaborately patterned socks. It was more than likely that the socks he wore when "sitting" for MacLeay were made by himself.

Willie's nickname of "Beardie" was well-earned. In his younger days his hair and beard were black and magnificent, but the years took their toll of his whiskers. In 1865, when Queen Victoria stayed at Blair, she met Willie, "an old acquaintance". She remarked on the fact that he "had formerly a very long black beard and hair, which are now quite grey".

"Beardie" Duff was, like many other foresters of last century, highly individualistic, some almost to the point of eccentricity, like James Cattanach, who was nicknamed An Righ, the King. Cattanach, who came from Ardverikie, was described by A.I.M. McConnochie in *The Deer Forests of Scotland* as "a peculiar stalker". This King of the Stalkers, who served with the Duke of Leeds at Mar Lodge on Deeside, never spoke unless it was absolutely necessary – and never consulted anyone.

His greatest peculiarity was that he refused to crawl in the heather – a dislike he shared with Prince Albert, who had the ditch dug on the Balmoral estate so that he could "stalk" deer from it without getting down on his knees. Cattanach's technique was straightforward. He simply walked ahead of the shooting party and pointed his stick towards the stag to be shot.

Then there was William Macdonald, who, like John Crerar, became a subject for one of Landseer's paintings, *The Bringing Home of the Deer*. William, who died in Glenmore in 1850, was said to be the last of the sun-worshippers. Every morning he went to a grassy hillock, bowed towards the sun, and said his prayers. His only explanation was that his father had done the same thing.

Burns's "brother catguts" could be found all over the Grampians. Some, like John Cameron, from Glenmuick, were itinerant fiddlers, taking their music through the glens to other communities. Up in Loch Lee, in the far reaches of Glenesk, the people often gathered to listen to "the fascinating music of a celebrated performer on the violin". This was Cameron, who came over the Mounth for over forty years to entertain the folk of Glenesk, arriving about the beginning of December and often finding it impossible to return home until the snow-choked glens had cleared.

Cameron belonged to Crathie and must have known Willie Blair, the Queen's official fiddler. He was taught by Peter Hardie, who was a gamekeeper with the Duke of Atholl, and is thought to have studied with Niel Gow.

Willie, who liked a dram, was often plied with drink when he played at Deeside functions, with the result that the minister of Crathie Kirk warned him to be careful of over-indulgence. On his way home from a dance he would look in on the minister and tell him, "I jist came in on my wye hame so that ye micht see me, in case ye should hear I wis waur nor I am". The whisky never did Willie any harm – like John Crerar, he lived to be over 90.

Today, the old-style fiddlers have vanished from the scene, but the foresters, the keepers, are still there. For them, however, things are not the same as they were in the days of men like John Crerar and "Beardie" Duff. Willie Forbes, who was head-keeper on the Mar Lodge estate for many years, thinks that times have changed for the stalker, particularly if he works, not for a laird, but for a proprietor who runs an estate as a commercial concern. "People pay a lot of money for a week's sport," he said. "They want stalking every day."

Some want more than their share. George Rafferty, the Grantown "vet" whose TV series put Speyside on the map, told in his book *The Vet* about an irascible Colonel Oliver Haig, on the Inchrory estate, who thought that his paying guests had shot more birds than they should have done. Next day, the Colonel locked them in their rooms like naughty children so that they would lose a day's sport.

It may be that the "characters" have gone. One of the last of that rare breed was Bob Scott, of Luibeg, on the edge of the Cairngorms, who died in 1981. He was a legendary figure, still spoken of by hundreds of hillwalkers and climbers who came to know him over the years. His cottage stood near the now ruinous Derry Lodge, and his

Bob Scott's cottage at Luibeg, on the edge of the Cairngorms.

bothy, which was burned to the ground a few years ago, was home to hundreds of climbers and hillwalkers.

While proprietors tend to look on hillwalkers with distrust, many keepers show a much greater degree of tolerance. Bob Scott was one of them. He was in the tradition of Alex Cameron, who was stalker at Allt-na-giubhsaich Lodge on the Balmoral estate for over twenty years. When he returned in 1905 the Cairngorm Club presented him with a gold watch in recognition of "his unfailing courtesy to all mountaineers who passed through his gate on the way to Lochnagar".

Estate owners have had to come to terms with the fact that more and more people are drawn to the hills. Glentanar estate, which was opened up to the public some years ago, has to cope each weekend with scores of people from Aberdeen and Deeside. There is a visitors' centre and walks are laid out for those who want to wander about the estate. One of the walks passes the lovely Chapel of St Lesmo, built in 1870 by its eccentric laird, Sir William Cunliffe-Brooks.

"W.C.B." was an enthusiastic hunter. The pews of the chapel are lined with deerskin and at one time deer antlers decorated the interior. They were removed when somebody decided that the horns of dead stags were hardly suitable adornments for the inside of a kirk. The millionaire owner lies in the private burial ground at St Lesmo, as does his old forester, Donald Mackintosh.

There is a large boulder at the foot of Donald's grave. It lay at one time in the hills above Glentanar and "W.C.B." and his keeper often sat by it when out shooting. They sometimes spoke about what would happen after they were gone, joking about who would die first, and Cunliffe-Brooks said he would arrange for the boulder to be put at the foot of the grave of the first one to go,

Donald died first and Sir William had the boulder taken down from the hill and set beside his forester's grave. He also had an inscription cut out in a stone at the top of the grave. Still there today, it reads "Deer Stalker – None Better". No keeper could have asked for a more fitting epitaph.

CHAPTER 10

THE
LAST
TRIP

THE LITTLE HAMLET OF DOWALLY sits on the edge of the A9 about five miles north of Dunkeld. It is the gateway to a vast tract of moorland stretching between Strathtay and Strathardle. Here, old tracks trace their intricate patterns through the hills and tiny lochans leap out of the heather to break the raw monotony of rock and juniper bush. It was in this area, south of Loch Ordie, that Queen Victoria lost her way while travelling south to Dunkeld in 1865, taking the wrong turning in the dark and pushing on in blinding rain while John Brown muttered about a road "full of holes and stones".

If you approach Dowally by the old north road from Dunkeld it will take you between Craigiebarns and a hill called the King's Seat – the old King's Pass, where Scottish monarchs are said to have taken potshots with their bows and arrows at deer being driven through the narrow pass. The pass itself is supposed to contain a gruesome reminder of the reason for Dowally's existence.

When Scotland was ravaged by plague in 1500, hundreds of people sought refuge in Dunkeld, drawn there by the hope that they would be safe in the Cathedral town. So many people converged on it that Bishop George Brown of Dunkeld, fearing that it would be overrun, settled the refugees in the river-haughs of Dowally, setting it up as a new parish with a church – a "long, narrow, inelegant structure" – to serve their religious needs.

Although the Bishop's move seems to have kept Dunkeld safe from infection, the plague took its toll of the refugees sent to Dowally. For many years a cairn marked the burial place of the settlers who died. When a new highway was opened up through the King's Pass to Ballinluig and Logierait, the men who worked on it were uneasy about building the road on the bones of Dowally's dead.

There is still a church at Dowally (pronounced Dowlie), built on the site of the old kirk and with the arms of Bishop Brown on its east wall. There is also a modern restaurant and crafts centre on its doorstep, so Dowally, which has always turned its back on the outside world (perhaps because the outside world turned its back on Dowally), is slowly being dragged into the tail-end of the twentieth century.

Friendly enough though they are, Dowally folk tend to be reticent with visitors, suspicious that their peace will be shattered and fearful that they will be engulfed in the new wave of tourism in Atholl. Perhaps they are remembering what happened when Dunkeld was overrun five centuries ago. They certainly have grounds for concern, for the empty acres at Loch Ordie and Loch Benachally are already being turned into a picnic playground by people from Dunkeld.

It is disturbing to think that this wild place might become the haunt of tourists, scattering their Coke cans and chocolate wrappers in the heather. Queen Victoria was the first tourist. They even built a cairn to commemorate her visit, for despite her unhappy introduction to the Dowally moors she went back to Loch Ordie with the Duchess of Athole and had a picnic under the trees. They rode there in a "sociable" (an open carriage with two seats facing each other), going by the Dowally and Rotmell lochs – the route they should have taken on their arrival.

This is a land of lochs. Between Dunkeld and Blairgowrie they drape the southern edge of the Forest of Clunie like a long cluster of pearls. They have names like Drumellie and Butterstone, Craiglush and Cally. The largest is the Loch of Lowes, which the Scottish Wildlife Trust runs as a nature reserve, with a visitor centre and a hide from which you can watch the courtship antics of great crested grebes and spot a dabchick among the white spikes of bogbean. Queen Victoria did a grand tour of the lochs, including the Loch of Lowes.

When the Queen was at Loch Ordie she "took a short row on it in a 'coble'". There were two cobbles at the water's edge when I was there, apparently used for fishing. Near the track from Dowally is the cairn commemorating the Queen's visit. From the Loch, tracks thrust north to more lochs, among them Pitcarmich Loch, where the Pitcarmich Burn runs east to join the River Ardle. It was at Pitcarmick Farm that Victoria and her party found ponies waiting to carry them south to Dunkeld.

It must have been Victoria's love of wild places that set her off on her pony trek through the country south of Kindrogan Hill. She could have travelled a good deal more comfortably by carriage, west to Pitlochry and down the main north road to Dunkeld. "At first there was a rough road", she wrote in her *Journal*, "but soon there was nothing but a sheep track, and hardly that, through heather and stones up a pretty steep hill". Mist lay over the moors and the rain poured down – "violently", said the Queen. They passed the twin Oisinneach lochs, arriving at Loch Ordie "dripping wet". There they had tea and whisky before going on to lose themselves in the woods north of Dunkeld.

Victoriana have become fashionable today, and some people think we get too much of them – the latest gimmick is to set up Victorian trails, taking tourists through the villages she visited (sometimes incognito) and past the grand houses she stayed in. Kincardine and Deeside Tourist Board have started the 'nineties by setting up a Victorian

Loch Ordie, where Queen Victoria took a short row in a "coble".

Heritage Trail – a signposted route from Fettercairn, where Victoria stayed at the Ramsay Arms, to Braemar. It is expected to become a major attraction on Deeside.

There are no Victorian trails going into the hills, yet the Queen was never happier than when she got off the beaten track, as she did in Atholl. She loved the wilderness areas, and she did more than most people to open up these Highland glens. Now, more than a century after that sodden pony ride to Loch Ordie, people are following in her footsteps, learning how to appreciate the land they live in.

It is happening in the lovely woodlands around Kindrogan Hill, where the aim of the Kindrogan Field Centre, near Enochdhu, is "to create a greater public awareness and understanding of the Scottish countryside". Here, where hundreds of students come to learn about everything from mountain flowers to the ecology of the Grampians, they unashamedly cash in on the Victorian link.

The Queen was joined at Pitmarich by "Mr Small Keir of Kindrogan", who found he couldn't keep up with "the immense pace of Brown and Fyvie" ("dear Fyvie," the

Queen's pony) and had to drop behind. Patrick Small Keir was the laird of Kindrogan. He was a close friend of the Circuit judge, Lord Cockburn, who often stayed at Kindrogan House ("a sensible house," he said) and thought that the household was kind and honest. "Let a friendly stranger go to Kindrogan and be unreasonable," wrote Lord Cockburn in 1841, "and he will know what true hospitality is."

The house was full of "friendly strangers" when I looked in on it. They were busy on a variety of courses, including one which would have delighted the heart of Beatrix Potter. It was called "Eating Fungi", and its aim was to teach students how to find fungi and identify them. From here, too, parties of students were going out to explore the old ways through the glens.

Kindrogan was purchased by the Scottish Field Studies Association as a residential centre in 1963. The oldest part of the building was built in the eighteenth century by William Small, an ancestor of Patrick's, but a new frontage and wings were added in the nineteenth century, Now there are four well-equipped laboratories in an extension at the rear of the building. So Kindrogan has one foot in the twentieth century and the other in the Victorian era – there is a walk in the grounds which passes a plaque marking the spot where the Queen "rested and partook of tea".

When the Queen went home to Balmoral after her 1865 trip to Dunkeld, she avoided the wild Loch Ordie route. Instead, she travelled up the main Pitlochry road, passing Little Dowally. Other tiny hamlets are spaced out along this route, many of them with the A9 traffic almost on their doorsteps. Guay, just a short distance beyond Dowally, is used to this sort of thing, although on a more modest, less noisy scale, for as far back as 1340 the Bishop of Dunkeld built a house there for travellers and visitors. Bishop Brown, who sent his refugees from the plague to Dowally, restored the house in 1490, but it was abandoned at the Reformation.

Kindallach is another hamlet on the A9 chain, one of a number of small communities that lie on a high wide shelf of land stretching from the Pass of Dunkeld to Moulin at Pitlochry. Through it runs an old road that swings east beyond Guay and Kindallachan to Tulliemet, and west again to Ballinluig, which looks across to Logierait, where the Tay and the Tummel meet.

Queen Victoria mentioned Logierait in her *Journal*, although she never actually visited it – "We saw the place where the monument to the Duke is to be raised". The monument – a huge Celtic-type cross – was built as a memorial to the 6th Duke of Atholl. Logierait is a historic place, taking its name from Lag an rath, the hollow of the castle, the castle belonging to Robert III. It was the seat of an Atholl court of regality. Rob Roy escaped from there in 1717, and Prince Charles dragged 600 prisoners all the way from Prestonpans to house them in the Logierait jail. Wordsworth stayed at an inn there in 1803.

There is, however, no monument to Logierait's female Falstaff. She was an eighteenth-century landlady who gave accommodation to William Gilpin, the English vicar who romped around the countryside writing books about his travels. In 1776, during a tour of Scotland, he landed up in Logierait and was sent to the boatman's home, a thatched hut where there was nothing but "dampness, dirt and disorder".

"Here sat the mistress of the family, with several of her children beside her. The good woman was dirty, black, and overgrown, and seemed just Sir John Falstaff in petticoats. The children were half-naked and dirty, but with health and cheerfulness in their looks." Gilpin asked for refreshment and a whisky bottle was produced, along with bread and cheese. The whisky was measured out by "a tin *stoup* which by frequent use, by the impression of the smoke, and by the religious reverence with which it had been kept sacred from anything like rinsing or washing, had assumed a hue something between dirty brown and a jet black."

Gilpin was then given a glass which "had lost its only leg and foot" and was thickly coated with a mixture of soot and dust. She kept the bottle in her lap, pouring so much to herself that Gilpin thought her liking for it must have "contributed largely to the enlargement of her bulk". Despite all this, the vicar was impressed by the family's health and hospitality – and, in the end, glad that he hadn't stayed "in a more commodious inn".

He might have fared better if he had gone on to Moulinearn, about two miles north of Logierait. Alfred Barnard, who visited Auchnagie Distillery near Tulliemet, said that in olden times it was customary for every traveller to stop at Moulinearn and have a glass of Athole brose. Queen Victoria maintained the tradition when she passed through the hamlet in 1844 – a glass of it was brought to her carriage.

Nowadays, Athole Brose is an expensive drink served up as a special treat at St Andrew's Night dinners. Barnard said that in Perthshire "the natives" had a high opinion of it, but he preferred whisky by itself or with "a small addition of the crystal stream from the hills". Like Barnard, I have never liked it much, which means I must be a pygmy among drinkers, for Sir Robert Bruce Lockhart, who was an expert on the subject, said it was "a giant's drink".

There are different recipes, but the one Sir Robert gave was to mix equal quantities of running heather honey and fine oatmeal in a little cold water, then slowly pour in well-flavoured malt whisky. Stir vigorously until a froth rises to the top, then bottle and cork tightly, keep for two days and "serve in the finest silver bowl that you possess". The silver seems to be important, for once I heard that you should stir the mixture with a silver spoon.

There were seven distilleries in Moulin parish at one time, but Victoria seems to have kept well clear of them. It is surprising that she didn't drop in on the distillery at Edradour, a picturesque little corner of Perthshire to the east of Pitlochry. "We left the Inverness road," the Queen wrote in her *Journal*, "and turned to the right up a very steep hill past Dunavourd (Mr Napier's, son of the historian), past Edradour (the Duke's property), over a wild moor."

At one time you could travel down that narrow, winding road and see little traffic, but not any more. It has become a whisky trail, drawing a steady stream of coaches to Edradour to see the smallest distillery in Scotland. It could probably also claim to be the most attractive distillery in Scotland, its whitewashed buildings tucked into a hollow by the Edradour Burn. It was founded by a group of local farmers in 1825 and is virtually unchanged since Victorian times. Alfred Barnard's only comment about it was that it was "not unlike a farmstead", which, I suppose, is true enough, but it deserved better from the Victorian whisky-chaser.

When Queen Victoria took the Edradour road on her way home from Dunkeld, she turned her back on an area crowded with memories. She avoided going through Pitlochry, but she could see it in the distance, bringing to mind the first time she had passed through it in 1842. Even in her wildest dreams she could never have imagined that this "small village" would blossom into a famous holiday resort – or that the Tummel valley would become the heartbeat of a scheme pouring power into the homes and factories of Scotland. During her 1866 visit she went to Loch Tummel and had a picnic on "a highish point called after me". It was the Queen's View, a spot that now draws thousands of visitors.

As she rode up the Edradour road, looking back towards the grey glimmer of the Tay, she thought of how twenty-four years earlier she and her party had gone sixteen miles up Loch Tay by boat – "with pibrochs playing and the boatmen singing wild Gaelic songs". She wrote in her *Journal* about Lord Breadalbane welcoming her to Taymouth Castle "in a princely style, not to be equalled for grandeur". Pipers played, guns fired, a great crowd cheered, and Highlanders lined the hall and stairs as the Royal couple arrived on their historic visit.

Twenty years before *that*, John Campbell, the 4th Earl of Breadalbane, had planned the same sort of reception for George IV, but the King had stayed in Edinburgh and Breadalbane had taken a house in St Andrew Square and filled it with fifty Campbells from Strathtay. Now, two decades later, the 2nd Marquess and 5th Earl – "dear Lord Breadalbane" – had set out to show what Royal Geordie had missed.

Victoria's journey back to Balmoral in 1866 took her through Glen Brerachan, past the gates of what Lord Cockburn called "nice, kindly Kindrogan", and south to Enochdhu and Kirkmichael, where the B950 links up with Dulrulzion in Glenshee. On her way to Dunkeld in 1865, Victoria followed the conventional route by Glenshee and Strathardle before turning into the hills south of Kindrogan. On her way home, she again abandoned the main roads and headed into the hills. Here again she was opening up a route that even today sees only keepers and hillwalkers.

"Huge clumsy mountains, bulk and loneliness" was how Lord Cockburn described the land north of Glen Brerachan. It is a vast, unwelcoming wilderness, broken by endless hills and slashed by remote and little-known glens. Near Enochdhu, a private road pushes deep into the heart of Atholl by Glen Fernate, stretching away to Fealer Lodge and Glen Tilt. The lodge is the highest in Scotland and probably the remotest.

From Enochdhu a track goes north-east to the Spittal of Glenshee. This was the way that Queen Victoria went, through the hills by what she called "the Larich" – the Lairig, or pass. "We turned over the hill, through a wild, heathery glen, and then up a grassy hill called the Larich, just above the Spittal. Looking back the view was splendid, one range of hills behind the other, of different shades of blue". When they reached the

Kindrogan House, described by Lord Cockburn as "nice, kindly Kindrogan".

summit they stopped for tea, but found that they had no kettle in which to make it. They sent one of the keepers two miles down to the Spittal to get one.

When Lord Cockburn was at the Spittal he found "a very nice inn – excellent eggs, butter, and oatcakes and milk". The inn is now a modern hotel catering for the hundreds of skiers who descend on this area during the winter. The old Spittal has been pushed into the background by the modern road that sweeps winter sports enthusiasts up Glen Beg to the Cairnwell.

The Spittal of Glenshee has been a wayside halt for centuries, back to the days when the original hospice served travellers making the dangerous journey over the Mounth from Deeside. Dreams and desperate deeds rub shoulders at the Spittal. Across the stream known as the Allt a' Ghlinne Bhig a path leads into the misty world of Celtic mythology. There is a farm shown on some maps as Tomb Farm and the farmer was at one time called Fear Tulaich Diarmid, the laird of Diarmid's Hill. This is where Diarmid O'duine, the hero of one of the great Fingalian legends, is said to be buried.

The glens stretch long arms into the hills from the Spittal. This was the way the cateran came. Cateran or reivers (they were also called "cleansers" because of the clean sweep they made on their raids) were a plague on the land. Early in the seventeenth century more than 2,500 cattle were driven off in a raid on Glenshee, Glenisla and Strathardle by raiders from Glen Garry.

In 1591 the Earl of Argyll was charged with raiding Glenisla. His son "murthorit all the inhabitants they could lay their hands on and took spulzie (spoils), including a

118

grit nowmor of nolt, schiep, etc…" but although they were pronounced rebels, there is no record that they were taken before the Privy Council. They came from the north and west, from upper Argyll, Badenoch and Lochaber. They went over the northern shoulder of Ben Gulbeine or Gulabin, which stands above the Spittal of Glenshee, to Rhidorrach, the highest sheiling on the Cairnwell road, and from these across the eastern ridge into Glen Brighty, which opened the way by Tulchan to Glenisla.

The route, which was still known last century as the Caterans' Road, touched Glen Taitneach, which branches off Glen Lochsie about a mile and a half from the Spittal. It was in Glen Taitneach that Donald Mor Campbell, the chief of the Lochaber cateran, was slain. Time ran out for him in 1665, when the Lochaber reivers were travelling home from raids on Glen Prosen and Glen Isla. Their pursuers caught up with them in Glen Taitneach, at the foot of the fairies' burn, Coire Sidh, when the morning mist still

The sculptures at Cairnwell survey the modern scene.

lay over their camp. In the brief encounter that followed Donald Mor was killed. He was buried in the Spittal churchyard and his funeral expenses were paid by "Little Eppie", wife of the host at the Spittal inn. She got her money back by selling Donald's clothes and silver buttons.

The ancient pass over the Cairnwell from the Spittal of Glenshee was once known as Carnavalage, the name given to it by Sir James Balfour of Denmylne in his list of eleven main routes over the mountains from the River Tay to the River Dee. The relics of the martyred St. Andrew came over this pass to be received by Angus I MacFergus, King of the Picts, who built a chapel to Scotland's patron saint in the Dee valley.

The drovers came this way, the cattle raiders behind them, watching and waiting in the shadowed glens, and it was here that General Wade's successors cut their way through the hills to build a military road from Blairgowrie to Grantown-on-Spey. Some of the old "Wade" bridges still stand as a monument to that massive work. A passing parade of Royalty went over what Queen Victoria described as the "very fine pass called Cairn Wall". Finally, the first spluttering motor car struggled up that nightmare double hairpin bend known as the Devil's Elbow.

I have often wondered who gave it that name. Frantic drivers, watching the steam rising from their tortured radiators, must often have thought that they had the De'il in the passenger seat. Back in the 1920s, the Cairnwell road was a rough rubble surface of sharp stones and blind corners where the road bent to take the curves of the hill. In 1930, in a book called *Fair Perthshire*, the author, Hamish Miles, said that both the surface and the gradient had been made less exacting, although to engines and drivers it remained a "formidable feat".

"Nothing," he added, "can abolish the headlong view down the steep gully which the unaccustomed traveller is apt to find unnerving as the car creeps round the edge of its rim. Still, who would welcome the straightening out of the 'Elbow'? The risk, or at least the sense of risk, adds spice to the fact that we are now on the highest stretch of main road in the British Isles."

Well, the Elbow was straightened out, but it is a pity that the old road wasn't left to become an alternative tourist route. It would have been particularly popular in summer, when the snow has gone. In winter, when ski-ing is in full swing, there are enough cars; too many, in fact. Very often the gates have to be closed at Cairnwell because the car parks are full.

The road to Glen Cluny passes between the Cairnwell (3,059 ft) and Glas Maol (3,502 ft). If you climb up from the ski centre, past the untidy clutter of tow lines, it will take you across Glas Maol to Caenlochan and the old Monega Pass, which drops down into Strathmore. Farther down Glen Cluny a Scottish Rights of Way Society sign indicates another approach to Monega Hill by Sron na Gaoithe.

Caenlochan Glen is a naturalist's paradise. Professor William MacGillvray, Professor of Natural History at Aberdeen's Marischal College, whose *Natural History of Deeside and Braemar* became a classic, did his early botanical explorations at Caenlochan in the early and mid-years of last century. His book was published by Queen Victoria after his death.

Queen Victoria went to Caenlochan – "a bonnie place" – on one of her Great Expeditions, climbing up from Loch Callater and crossing the plateau to what she called the "Month Eigie Road". There is a well-known picture of Victoria and Albert having lunch on the edge of Caenlochan. "We sat on a very precipitous place," she wrote in her diary, "which made one dread any one's moving backwards." It must have been a chilly meal, for up on that great tableland the Royal explorers found ice thicker than a shilling. John Brown took a piece in his hand and was unable to melt it.

The Monega expedition, when the Queen rode up Glen Callater on a bright, frosty morning on her faithful pony "Fyvie", must have lain closest to her heart. It took place in October, 1861, and two months later Prince Albert was dead. In 1867, when the Queen's *Journal* was due to be published, she added one final sentence to her account of the expedition. It read – "Alas! I fear our *last* great one!"

*   *   *   *   *

FURTHER READING

Brander, Michael, *A Hunt Around the Highlands*. Standfast Press, 1973.

Burgess, Rosemary and Robert Kinghorn, *Speyside Railways*. Aberdeen University Press, 1988.

Clark, Ronald W., *Balmoral*. Thames and Hudson, 1981.

Cooper, Derek, *The Whisky Roads of Scotland*. Jill Norman and Hobhouse Ltd., 1982.

Duff, David, *Queen Victoria's Highland Journals*. Webb and Bower, 1980.

Eden, Ronald, *Going to the Moors*. John Murray, 1979.

Fraser, Amy Stewart, *The Hills of Home*. Routledge and Kegan Paul, 1973; *In Memory Long*, 1977; *Roses in December*, 1981.

Gibson, Colin, *Highland Deerstalker*. Culross, 1958.

Hart-Davis, Duff, *Monarchs of the Glen: A History of Deer-stalking in the Scottish Highlands*. Jonathan Cape, 1978.

Lennie, Campbell, *Landseer: The Victorian Paragon*. Hamish Hamilton, 1976.

Moss, Michael and Hume, John, *Old Photographs from Scottish Country Houses*. Hendon Publishing Company Ltd., Nelson, Lancs., 1980.

Neil, Catherine G., *Glengairn Calling*. Aberdeen University Press, 1943.

Ormond, Richard, with contributions by Joseph Rishel and Robin Hamlyn. *Sir Edwin Landseer*. Thames and Hudson in association with the Philadelphia Museum of Art and the Tate Gallery, London, 1981.

Prebble, John, *The King's Jaunt*. Collins, 1988.

The Scottish Annual and the Braemar Gathering Book. Herald Press, Arbroath, 1987.

Tranter, Nigel, *The Queen's Scotland*. Hodder and Stoughton, 1972.

Wyness, Fenton, *Royal Valley: The Story of the Aberdeenshire Dee*. Reid, 1968.

INDEX